ROLE-PLAY
A Practical Guide

ROLE-PLAY

A
PRACTICAL
GUIDE

ELLICE MILROY

ABERDEEN UNIVERSITY PRESS

First published 1982
Aberdeen University Press
A member of the Pergamon Group

© Ellice Milroy 1982

British Library Cataloguing in Publication Data

Milroy, Ellice
  Role-Play: a practical guide
  1. Education—simulation methods
  2. Role playing
  I. Title
  371.3   LB1029.S53

  ISBN 0-08-025744-5
  ISBN 0-08-025745-3 Pbk

PRINTED IN GREAT BRITAIN
AT THE UNIVERSITY PRESS
ABERDEEN

CONTENTS

PREFACE   vii

ACKNOWLEDGEMENTS   viii

INTRODUCTION   ix

PART ONE   1
1   The Technique   2
2   Validity of Technique   33
3   Methods of Introducing the Device   45

PART TWO   67
1   Preparation for Teaching   68
2   Conversational Skills   91
3   Subject Teaching   127
4   School to Work   134
5   Youth and Community   141

PART THREE   163
1   Scripted Role-Play   164
2   Gaming   178

CONCLUSION   189

PREFACE

This book has been written to attract the attention of people who are, or might be, interested in methods of teaching based on simulation. The writer has in mind not only teachers in schools and colleges but also persons who are involved in training programmes outside the formal educational system.

The book is divided into three parts and into sections within each part.

Part One describes the technique of role-play and the functions of the person in charge who will be styled 'the tutor'. It attempts to identify some problems inherent in the device and in reactions to it and concludes with examples of ways in which role-play may be introduced to people unaccustomed to this method of learning.

In Part Two the application of role-play is examined in the context of different circumstances and programmes. The aim is to be as practical as possible and thus a wide variety of exercises is offered.

Part Three looks at the possibilities of scripted and recorded role-play, and of educational games.

It is never the intention of the writer to suggest that role-play and gaming are essential to the success of any programme of studies but it is hoped that the book will promote greater understanding of these techniques and of their possibilities and will provide material which, suitably adapted, may be helpful in training programmes for which readers are responsible.

The problem of the personal pronoun has been resolved by using 'he' on some occasions, 'she' on others, and occasionally 'he or she'. It is hoped by so doing to make clear that no discrimination is intended.

ACKNOWLEDGEMENTS

This book has as its origin work done over many years with groups of students mainly within the School of Community Studies, Moray House College of Education, Edinburgh.

Being convinced of the educational value of techniques based on simulation, the writer used role-play in a variety of teaching programmes. Because of the attitude of students in response to role-play the writer became increasingly aware of both the limitations and the possibilities of this method of working. She would like, therefore, to acknowledge with thanks the contribution which students made to the information contained within this book.

INTRODUCTION

Central to the understanding of role-play is an appreciation of the concept of *role* upon which the technique is based. Role-theory is complex, and we are concerned at present only with aspects necessary for the understanding of role-play.

ROLE

There are several viewpoints from which human behaviour may be examined. The perspective of the sociologist seems to be the study of the behaviour of the individual who is in action with others in the context of a particular social system. The sociologist seeks to analyse this inter-personal behaviour through the concept of *role*.

During the course of a single day a person may occupy several social positions, for instance those of mother, wife, social worker, friend; or to take another example, brother, son, teacher, colleague. In any one of these positions the occupant relates to others in an associated position. For example, a mother relates to children; wife to husband, social worker to clients, friend to friend and so on. The way one behaves in each relationship stems, fundamentally, from the position one occupies. Thus mother-type behaviour towards a child is different in important respects from social worker-type behaviour towards a client, and both types of behaviour differ again from that which would obtain in a friend-to-friend relationship. The sociological term for position behaviour is *role*.

As a mother relates to a child, so the child relates to the mother. The child is the *pair-role* in the mother/child relationship and vice versa. If one looks at a person in his family role of father and, also, in his work role of teacher, it will be apparent that a son (or daughter) will expect father-type behaviour at home but pupils in school will not expect father-type behaviour when the position of teacher is assumed. Even if the father-cum-teacher meets his son-cum-pupil in school both will expect from each other behaviour appropriate to the different circumstances.

A social role, therefore, may be defined as behaviour expected of a person by virtue of the position he or she is occupying.

Expectations are not confined only to those of pair-roles. For instance, in our example, the particular school will expect our teacher to behave within certain limits, and society at large also has ideas of how the role of teacher should be played. Whether or not an individual teacher chooses to conform to an expected pattern is a matter of personal choice. Nevertheless, should a teacher's concept of the role be so far removed from what is expected, that teacher may run into trouble of a temporary or permanent nature.

LEARNING TO PLAY A ROLE

Sociologists place roles in three groups—Social, Family and Work. Each group is considered separately and briefly.

Learning to play a social role starts from birth. By the very fact that a baby is born into a particular society he or she has to learn to behave in terms of that society. Thus the baby learns the language in common usage and acquires other aspects of behaviour acceptable to the society into which he or she has been born.

There are different phases in this learning process and there are people and factors that affect socialisation. Because the baby is born with the capacity to learn to be social he or she will respond to external stimuli and thus to a considerable extent will be his or her own learning agent. Of course socialisation is an ongoing process and as the individual grows older he assumes certain social roles for which no necessary or conscious training is expected of him, but how he chooses to play these roles will be governed by the laws of the land, expectations of pair-roles, his attitude to these matters and his own personality. Thus, although no training is required for the roles of, for example, neighbour, citizen and senior citizen, individual role-performances vary. If in the performance of a role an individual breaks the law of the land the appropriate penalty is exacted.

LEARNING TO PLAY A FAMILY ROLE

A child is also a son (or daughter) and he learns to play this role through his association with his parents and his observation of other son/parent relationships. The amount of conscious training a child undergoes varies according to the wishes and expectations of parents. The extent to which a child is prepared to submit to training varies also from child to child and according to the age and stage.

No conscious preparation or training is expected of intending occupants of new adult family roles. Nevertheless, much information on the playing of a specific role will have been accumulated from pair-role experience, from observation and perhaps also from other sources such as written material and television. A daughter, for instance, as pair-role in the mother/daughter relationship will be gathering information which she will draw on when she becomes a mother. She may also choose to augment knowledge through her own reading and/or attendance at preparation classes.

There are restrictions which society places upon behaviour but within limits how a person chooses to play a family role is largely a matter of personal preference, commitment and capability.

WORK ROLES

For the majority of work roles a period of training of one kind or another is required during which intending occupants must acquire necessary qualifications/skills to permit them to play the chosen work role.

ROLE-CHANGE

In life man plays his different roles and moves from one to another adjusting behaviour accordingly, and particularly if roles are familiar ones, with little or no conscious thought. In the course of living, however, man chooses new roles or has new roles thrust upon him. When required to play a new role it can be difficult coming to an understanding of the obligations and responsibilities and then adjusting behaviour to try to meet them. Most would agree that when a daughter becomes a wife, or a husband a father, adjustments in behaviour are necessary and not always easily accomplished. Similarly the employed person made unemployed either through redundancy or age has to make alterations in behaviour stemming from the role-change which may not be welcomed or easily made.

At the other end of the chronological scale, the moves from child to adolescent and adolescent to adult present problems for those who are making the change and pair-roles affected by the change. Parents, for example, can experience some difficulty adjusting their behaviour from that previously required in the parent/child relationship to what is expected of them in the new relationship of parent to adolescent.

ROLE-PERFORMANCE

How a person performs in a new role may depend upon motivation, aptitude, application and the extent and nature of the interest in or preparation for, the role.

Performance is likely to be affected also by the support and encouragement of more experienced occupants and, most importantly, by the expectations and attitude of relevant pair-roles.

As the responsibilities and requirements of a role become familiar so it is likely that the role-performance will become increasingly confident and assured.

I have tried to summarise role-theory in the context of the declared aims of this book. Let us now look at the implications.

If all children experienced few problems in the process of growing up and if all adolescents found it easy to become a member of adult society there would be no need to pay any special attention to adjustment. But they do not.

If new family roles were assumed with attendant problems easily faced and overcome there would be no point in giving such matters any special attention. But, again this does not happen.

If understanding of theory and apprenticeship training were sufficient to ensure effective role-performance there would be no need to look further into the problem of helping people to find their feet in a new job.

As the role-player operates not in isolation but in conjunction with the relevant pair-role(s) so the reciprocal nature of role-performance has to be acknowledged. It has to be accepted that theoretic understanding of the requirements of any role and necessary personal skills for the playing of the role, can be set at naught if there is no complementary knowledge of, and skill in, human relationships.

In illustration of this point follow, in imagination, a young newly qualified teacher as she sets out for her first post. Questions form in her mind and, as she gets nearer and nearer the school, tensions mount. But our young friend is determined not to show her anxiety and so she enters the building with firm step. She meets new colleagues and is taken by one of them to be introduced to her first class. Her colleague leaves the room and she is alone with the pupils.

In the setting of that particular classroom, teacher and pupils interact. The setting, the persons, what is said, what done, felt or thought—all of that is reality. Teacher and pupils are now engaged with each other in the building up of a relationship which will have significant effect upon the learning that takes place in the classroom. The teacher will hope so to motivate a particular group of pupils that they will wish to address themselves to the task of acquiring the particular knowledge or skills of the given lesson.

The effectiveness of our young teacher will hinge upon her pupil-management skills. Such skills are not acquired from study but are developed as knowledge is applied in the practical situation of the classroom. There is therefore the gap between knowing what to do and doing it. This gap is very familiar to all young people as they assume their chosen work role for the first time.

In the following pages I am concerned to give information about a technique which attempts to narrow the gap. It is called *role-play*, thus borrowing the sociological terminology.

Let us, therefore, proceed to describe the technique and consider its application.

PART ONE

Part One is divided into three sections.

Sections One and Two are concerned mainly with description.

The first section opens with two examples of role-play and closes with five further examples. Questions fundamental to the understanding of the technique are posed and answered.

In the second section, some doubts about the validity of role-play as a teaching tool are examined.

In the final section advice and suggestions are offered for the introduction of role-play to people unfamiliar with the technique.

THE TECHNIQUE

The sociological concept of role upon which role-play is based was summarised in the introduction. The technique is now described in practical terms, by means of two examples of role-play.

FIRST EXAMPLE

This example is intended to demonstrate the build-up to, and the organisation of, a simple role-play.

The tutor in this example is conducting a basic course on Interviewing with a group of twelve first-year social and community work students. The average age of the students is 19 and although all have done some fieldwork prior to entering college none has any experience as an interviewer.

In the first lesson students were given an opportunity to:
define an interview
draw a distinction between an interview and a social conversation
identify different types of interviews.

In the second lesson the following training objectives were outlined:
to consider questions and questioning
to use role-play to give practice in the framing and posing of questions in the context of an interview.

It was established that a major function of an interviewer is to collect information through a system of question and answer. Build-up to the role-play proceeded along the following lines.

Four types of questions were identified:

Closed:	a question that may be answered in one word.
Open:	one that encourages a fuller reply.
Leading:	a limiting question in that it invites a one word reply and/or suggests the answer.
Multiple:	a combination of two or more questions.

In discussion it was agreed that examples of each type of question were to be found in most interviews. The exception of a survey-type interview was acknowledged. It was acknowledged also that a complicated multiple question often leads to confusion.

Students were asked to give an example of a closed question and to re-frame it as OPEN and then LEADING. An example of a multiple question was also requested.

Sample

Closed:	Did you enjoy school?
Open:	Would you tell me about your schooldays?
Leading:	Was it because you changed school so often that you didn't enjoy yourself?
Multiple:	What were your favourite subjects at school and what clubs did you join and could you say if you have kept on any of these interests since leaving school?

After further discussion on clarity, word selection and the encouragement of desired response to questioning, the group was ready to tackle the role-play exercise.

ORGANISATION

Stages: briefing, interaction, discussion.

BRIEFING

The following information was given to the students by the tutor.

1. The situation is that an interview has been arranged between two persons for the purpose of gaining certain information which the interviewer requires for a class project.

2. To carry out this task please pair-off and then decide who is A and who B. Each pair will undertake the task. Interviews will proceed simultaneously. (Students paired off as requested and agreed who would be A and who B.)

3. Roles: As will be the interviewers, Bs will be the interviewees.

4. As. You are students who have an individual class project for which you are seeking information.
   Bs. You should choose your own role from your fieldwork experience. For instance some of you worked in a Children's Home so you could choose your role from that setting.

5. As will interview their own B in his or her chosen role.

6. Additional information. (i) Bs know that the student coming to see them is working on a class project the nature of which has not yet been disclosed. (ii) Arrangements were made by letter and telephone. (iii) Interviewer and interviewee did not meet, and do not know each other. (iv) Interviews will be conducted at the interviewee's place of work.

7. Further instructions. You have now ten minutes for preparation. There will be items of information which you will need to share, e.g. the role B has chosen and any other details that would have been given out when meeting was arranged. When the common knowledge is agreed, make your own preparation independently.

During the ten-minute preparation the tutor moved round ready to answer any queries or give requested help. After the preparation, the interviews began.

INTERACTION

During interaction the tutor moved round, observing each pair at work but taking care not to distract or influence them. Some interviewers had a set of questions which they put to interviewees. Two interviewers recorded replies to their questions, the others did not. One pair seemed to struggle from the beginning but the tutor did not intervene. One of the interviewers who had used prepared questions came to an abrupt end when his questions ran out.

   When it seemed as if interviewers had finished, the tutor stopped the inter-action.

DISCUSSION

Students, in pairs, were asked to discuss what transpired in their own interview and to try to note strengths and weaknesses. The group then reassembled and reports were given. Comments included:

1. I had a prepared set of questions and when I ran out I found I couldn't think of anything more to ask.

2. Our interview went very well at first but we thought in the end that we were just having a conversation.

3. The questions which my interviewer put were very clear but they jumped from topic to topic.

4. I used a lot of closed questions. I didn't intend to, but in fact this did not matter because the interviewee was so willing to talk that I got all the information I wanted.

5. I knew that I was being interviewed for a class project and so I wondered why my interviewee wasn't taking notes. We discussed this afterwards and decided that if you are going to take down what an interviewee actually says you should ask permission first of all.

6. I don't think ours went very well. I found it difficult to think up a project and so when the interview started I just didn't know what I was supposed to be doing. In the end we just talked about fieldwork.

7. I found it difficult to listen to replies as I was so busy thinking out my next question.

8. We decided that preparation was important but the interviewer should be able to follow any leads from interviewee and not stick too closely to his own questions.

9. Once or twice I was asked a multiple question. It's quite difficult to know which part of the question to answer first of all and by the time you've done that you've forgotten the other bits.

10. During the interviews we never thought about types of questions except once when I asked a leading question and got the expected answer. If I'd got an unexpected answer that might have thrown me.

The discussion closed with a summary of the lessons learned.

Teaching Points

1. Knowledge was acquired and then tested out in role-play.

2. Information concerning the simulated situation and the roles was made clear *before* interaction began.

3. The roles assumed by students who were to be interviewed were one of their own choosing within a limit set by tutor.

4. The tutor tried to ensure that everyone understood the task and had sufficient information to undertake it.

5. Not having a role within the simulated situation, the tutor took no part in the interaction other than as an observer.

6. Students were encouraged to comment on their own work.

7. Training issues were summarised.

SECOND EXAMPLE

The benefits to be derived from interaction hinge upon work done in the briefing stage of a role-play. To illustrate the truth of that statement the following example is offered.

The tutor in the exercise had been invited to take part in a residential course for school leavers, all of whom had major hearing loss. The tutor's contribution to the course extended over three days in all of the sessions she had the assistance of Youth and Community work students. Neither tutor nor students had a working knowledge of sign language.

On the first evening the session was concentrated upon communication through mime and gestures. In this world the tutor and her assistants were comparative strangers but the course students were in their element. Positions were therefore reversed. The course students realised that they were more skilled in the various games than were those who could hear. Who then were handicapped? This was an important question to pose and an essential one in the building up of confidence and self esteem.

The two sessions on the second day were devoted to role-play and were intended to give information on 'being interviewed for a job' and then to practise behaviour.

TUTOR'S PREPARATION

1. A series of flash cards 18×12in were prepared. These carried written explanations, definitions, instructions. A few samples may be sufficient to indicate the total briefing:

    (i) QUESTION—WHAT IS AN APPLICANT?
    ANSWER—THE NAME BY WHICH A PERSON
    APPLYING FOR A JOB IS KNOWN.

    (ii) THE EMPLOYER IS THE INTERVIEWER. PERSONS
    WANTING THE JOB ARE APPLICANTS.

    (iii) PLEASE WRITE DOWN ONE THING AN EMPLOYER
    MAY NOTICE ABOUT APPLICANTS HE INTERVIEWS.
    FOR EXAMPLE—CLEAN HANDS.

    (iv) EMPLOYERS WANT PEOPLE WHO WORK IN THEIR
    FIRMS TO GET ON WELL WITH EACH OTHER.

    (v) YOU ARE GOING TO SEE THREE INTERVIEWS.

    (vi) THE JOB IS TYPIST.

    (vii) THE EMPLOYER IS MR BLACK, WHO SITS IN HIS
    OFFICE.

    (viii) YOU HAVE TO DECIDE WHO GETS THE JOB.

2. The tutor met with members of her teaching team. Role-play demonstrations were discussed and the behaviour of applicants agreed on.
    First applicant—shy and generally lacking in confidence.
    Second applicant—confident and alert.
    Third applicant—unsmiling, over-confident.

Also discussed were the method of evaluation and the follow-up work.

3. Three additional flash cards were prepared;

    (i) APPLICANTS ARE MISS WHITE: MISS GREEN:
    MISS BROWN. (actual names of students were given)

    (ii) EACH OF YOU PUT A MARK √ BESIDE THE NAME
    OF THE APPLICANT WHO GETS THE JOB. IF YOU
    WANT TO, GIVE REASON FOR YOUR CHOICE.

    (iii) PLEASE DO THIS NOW.

4. All the flash cards were placed in sequence.

AT THE COURSE

The tutor, with the help of an interpreter, talked with course members to re-establish contact and to discover the extent of their knowledge of selection interviews.

BRIEFING

Briefing was undertaken through the medium of the flash cards. In turn each card was displayed and as each card was held up the message on it was spoken by the tutor. Course students were able to read and lip-read given information. Tutor checked with interpreter to try to ensure that students were understanding the briefing.

The briefing completed, the flash card bearing the names of applicants was fixed to a blackboard.

Mr Black, Miss White, Miss Green and Miss Brown were identified.
Mr Black set up his office.
The three applicants left the room.
When Mr Black was ready, the tutor now in the role of his secretary called the first applicant into the room, and the demonstration began.

INTERACTION

The three interviews took place as agreed. Each role-play was watched with great attention and much enjoyment.

EVALUATION

After the final interview these flash cards were displayed:

(i) EACH OF YOU PUT A MARK √ BESIDE NAME OF APPLICANT WHO GETS THE JOB. IF YOU WANT TO, GIVE REASON FOR YOUR CHOICE.
(ii) PLEASE DO THIS NOW.

Result: 2 marks for Miss White   word added : *shy*
7 marks for Miss Green   words added : *smiled; alert.*
2 marks for Miss Brown   words added : *nervous; long-faced.*

FOLLOW-UP WORK

The four members of the teaching team who had taken part in the demonstrations each took two or three course students and involved them in role-play. At first the role of employer was taken by the team member in every case but afterwards in one of the groups this role was taken successfully by a course student.

DE-BRIEFING

Back in college the tutor and the students met to discuss the sessions.

OBSERVATIONS

The course students were all deaf.

The tutor and members of the teaching team were handicapped in communication with the students. A method of briefing combining the written and spoken word was used. The course students greatly enjoyed role-playing. Tutors with no difficulty communicating to people who are deaf would not require to use flash cards. They might find their pupils/students would also enjoy role-playing and derive benefit from so doing.

WHAT IS ROLE-PLAY?

Role-play is a method of learning. The method is based on role-theory. Participants adopt assumed positions and interact in a simulated life situation. This occurs for some educational purpose, usually under the guidance of the person with the educational responsibility. The interaction is spontaneous and at its conclusion there is opportunity for discussion.

For what specific purposes would role-play be used?

A variety of purposes. Among the most common are:
(1) to put theoretic knowledge into practice
(2) to consider the responsibilities and obligations of specific roles
(3) to give practice in the playing of roles
(4) to promote greater awareness of the behaviour of pair-roles
(5) to promote more effective decision-making
(6) to stimulate discussion
(7) to clarify particular issues
(8) to study specific problems

Can role-play be used to solve problems?

If by solving problems one means providing participants with ready-made solutions applicable in life, then the answer is No. On the other hand, if one means, can role-play be used to promote more effective decision-making? then the answer is Yes. Role-play can be used to help participants arrive at their own solutions to a given problem. Even in such circumstances, however, emphasis would be not only upon Solutions but also on the process by which decisions were reached, and on other options and possible consequences.

Can role-play be used for therapeutic purposes?

Yes, it can, *but* it should be so used *only* by those who are professionally qualified to be in charge. People may quibble about the phrase 'for therapeutic purposes'. Obviously any experience can be a therapeutic one and role-play can have therapeutic value but readers will understand that there is a difference between 'having therapeutic value' and for 'therapeutic purposes'. It cannot be emphasised too strongly that the use of role-play in therapy should be confined to medical and allied professions. The person in charge of role-play should not allow interaction to develop beyond his or her own understanding and professional competence. Role-play is a method of learning that involves people in the interactive process for educational purposes and it is with that definition only that this book is concerned.

How is role-play organised?

A single role-play has three stages: Briefing; Interaction: Discussion

BRIEFING
During this stage the role-play is set up. That is to say:
(1) the simulated situation is chosen
(2) roles within that situation are determined
(3) the situation is explained
(4) roles are allocated
(5) all necessary information is assembled
(6) observers, if any, have their function explained.

INTERACTION
Interaction is the second stage. It is the playing out of the simulated situation. This playing is the spontaneous give-and-take behaviour of role-takers in their response to altering circumstances.

During interaction any observers look, listen and note what is happening. They do not influence interaction. On the contrary, observers remain detached from it.

Interaction may continue until the role-players have come to some conclusion but it can be stopped at any time either by one of the participants or by the person in charge. It is difficult to say when interaction should be stopped but as a useful guide interaction has served its purpose if sufficient learning points have been made. It could then be stopped. Certainly, if interaction is beginning to stray into areas outwith training objectives or if any participant is experiencing undue stress, interaction should be stopped. This matter will be dealt with more fully when considering functions of the tutor.

DISCUSSION

This is the third and often most valuable stage in a role-play. Those who were involved in the interaction and any who were observing join with the tutor to discuss matters that stemmed from interaction relevant to the educational purpose for which the role-play was designed. In particular they might consider:

(1) Decisions that were taken
(2) Possible consequences of decisions
(3) Other options open to interactants
(4) Aspects of behaviour that were rewarding/unrewarding
(5) Points that perhaps might be carried over into life situations of a similar nature.

Does the presence of observers create difficulties for the Role-players?

Yes, this can be so. Undoubtedly, and especially initally, the presence of observers can be inhibiting and can contribute to the alleged artificiality of the situation. This is an important question and will be discussed in detail in the section on *Methods of Introducing Role-play to Persons Unfamiliar with the Device.* Suffice it to say meantime that, in order to minimise the inhibiting effect of observers, tutors should set a first role-play that involves all members of the group in the interaction, and thus no one has the feeling of being observed. If, for some reason, that were not possible there would be need to explain the function of observers and during interaction to exercise some control over behaviour to eliminate as far as possible conduct appropriate in the theatre but not for observers of role-play.

When people gain confidence in themselves and in the company of others in the group, roles are assumed, and during interaction observers are forgotten— they have no influence. During discussion, the impression that observers have had of the interaction contributes greatly to the learning process and this is precisely what those who have played the roles come to appreciate.

All that being said, is it not really very difficult to persuade people to take part?

This is another question which will be discussed at a later stage. Briefly, how-ever, the answer is yes. It can be exceedingly difficult. It is so important that the tutor should know for what specific purposes the device is being introduced and what the chances are that this rather public method of learning will appeal to the tutorial group. To be vague on objectives or to try to use role-play in circumstances that are unfavourable for whatever reason is counter-productive. Sometimes, however, a seemingly antagonistic attitude can spring from lack of self-confidence and not from any deep-rooted dislike or distaste for acting in front of others. It should be recognised also, that certain other factors affect the desire to participate and therefore make persuasion comparatively easy or conversely quite difficult. In the present writer's experience the bigger the group, the wider the age-range, the more diverse in occupation and life-style are members of the group, and the greater are the feelings of apprehension that are engendered. Consequently the more difficult does the task of persuasion become. Significant, too, is the relationship between group and tutor. In the end, willingness to become involved probably depends more upon the confidence that members have in the tutor than upon any other factor. The tutor, therefore, in his or her own personality and *modus operandi* influences decisions that members will make.

In addition, the experience of each individual tutor will help him or her to recognise whether it might be wiser to choose another method of working or to press forward with role-play through perhaps an initial sticky beginning for the possible ultimate advantages to be gained. Certainly, tutors who choose to introduce role-play to others should be prepared for both pro and con reactions and should try to appreciate something of the feelings that prompted them.

What is the basic difference between presenting a problem to a group for discussion and presenting that same problem for role-play? Surely involvement can be as great in the former method as in the latter?

Yes, of course, commitment to the task can be as great in one method as in the other but there is one essential difference in the nature of the involvement. In a discussion people talk *about* the problem and in role-play people *assume that the problem is theirs* and interact on that assumption. Even in the discussion stage of role-play observations stem from how the people who had the problem coped not only with the problem *per se* but also with their own and other people's behaviour.

Is there more to be gained from one method than the other?

It is impossible to answer that question in terms other than—it all depends. The tutor would choose the method most likely to maximise learning. There is nothing inherently superior or inferior about the two ways of working. They are different.

What are the duties and responsibilities of the tutor?

This is a crucial question. It will be answered first by means of considering the tutor's duties and responsibilities in preparation for a training session and then in the three phases of a single role-play exercise. Five examples of role-play are offered in illustration of the method and of the tutor's functions.

THE TUTOR'S TASKS

PREPARATION

During preparation for a training session at which role-play is to be the teaching method, the tutor's first task is to determine educational objectives. He must then:

(i)   choose a situation that has relevance for members and is in line with objectives.

(ii)   determine roles within the simulated situation.

(iii) assemble information regarding the situation and the roles.

Notes

(i)   The information should be given in full when the tutor is in contact with students at the briefing.

(ii)   Information is of two kinds, intra- and inter-personal. Intra-personal information is what would be known to individual role-takers and therefore undeclared at the briefing but inter-personal information is the shared facts. For instance, in a staffroom all would know that Miss X was a new member of staff but only Miss X would know how she felt, although others might make an educated guess based on their own past experience.

(iii) All information relates to the past and brings role-takers to the point where interaction takes place.

BRIEFING

In the conduct of the briefing the tutor should:

(1) Outline educational objectives.

(2) Describe the simulated situation, trying to ensure that all relevant information is assembled. Give out prepared facts regarding situation, and through discussion establish other details.
(3) Declare the roles. Cast people in the different roles.
(4) Describe the roles. Gather in necessary additional inter-personal information.
(5) Give opportunity for role-takers to establish their own intra-personal information.
(6) Make all necessary other arrangements for the setting-up of the role-play, including arrangement of furniture or maybe a role-taker leaving the room to enter during interaction.

Notes

A tutor should try to ensure that people understand what they are being asked to do and for what purposes. This refers also to any observers of the interaction. If a person lacks information about a situation or a role he is being asked to play, that person may well refuse to take part. Alternatively, he may do so and, by calling upon his imagination and dramatic skill, give a performance that could be highly entertaining but quite improbable. This in its turn could convey to observers an impression of role-play that either confirmed their previously held opinions about the device and/or made their own participation most unlikely. The effectiveness of role-play, therefore, hinges upon the choice of situation and upon the briefing. If the former has little relevance for, or is outwith the experience of, role-takers and the latter is inadequate the exercise is likely at best to have only limited value and at worst to prejudice learning and perhaps also future relations between tutor and group.

INTERACTION

The tutor may have cast himself in a role in the simulated situation, in which case he is involved in the interaction on the same basis as the other role-takers. If the tutor is not a role-taker his function in this phase of the exercise is to *observe* interaction and be prepared to arrest or stop interaction for one or other of the following reasons:

(1) to support a role-taker who is experiencing undue stress;
(2) to support a role-taker who is finding the role difficult:
(3) to draw attention to aspects of the interaction deserving of comment.

Notes

(i) It should be appreciated that during interaction the tutor, unless he is involved as a role-player, does *nothing to influence behaviour*. Should it become obvious that a person is not coping with the given role, the tutor *must not take over* the role and in effect say, 'Watch me, I'll show you how the role should be played.' That action would defeat the purpose of a role-play which is to give people the opportunity to act individually on their own initiatives, make their own mistakes, and from so doing appreciate how they might do better in the future.

(ii) If a tutor considers that intervention is desirable;

(*a*) He can arrest interaction, lead out into discussion and then re-start role-play to give an opportunity for more effective playing. (This is illustrated in Example C which follows.)

(*b*) He can assume a role and in that role become involved in the interaction. For example, suppose that the role-play has been set to give practice in salesmanship. Early in the interaction it becomes obvious to the tutor that the person playing the role of the shop assistant is really struggling and finding it very difficult to cope with the customer pair-role. The tutor, assuming the role of supervisor, could move into the situation and say to the assistant something like, 'Excuse me, Miss Smith, can I be of assistance to you?' Then before she has time to reply he could turn to the customer and say, 'Miss Smith is one of our new assistants and this is her first day on the counter. Now, how may *we* help you?' At an appropriate moment thereafter he could either stop interaction and lead out into discussion or if he felt Miss Smith was beginning to cope, hand the customer back to her. In the subsequent discussion, issues such as problems of new assistants and the support they require from supervisors could be examined together with the all important question of manner in which any intervention on the part of the supervisor is made.

(*c*) Sometimes the best action is to stop interaction and proceed to discussion. If anyone is experiencing undue discomfort or if for some reason interaction is getting out of hand then it is advisable for the tutor to intervene. Whether or not he elicits comments from observers depends on his reasons for stopping interaction. The most appropriate action for the tutor to take in such circumstances may be to dismiss observers and confine the discussion to the role-takers.

(*d*) Sometimes it is a good idea to break into interaction and ask role-players to switch roles. Suppose someone is seeking to persuade another person to take a course of action and not succeeding very well. In such circumstances the tutor may arrest interaction and ask players to switch roles. (This device is styled role-reversal.) From the different viewpoint the original persuader may arrive at a better understanding of what is required in such an encounter.

DISCUSSION

The tutor's basic functions in this stage of role-play exercise are:

(1) to cause the different learning points to be identified.
(2) to help members put interaction into perspective.
(3) to encourage each individual member of the group to contribute to the discussion.
(4) to help members appreciate the insights and skills necessary for the effective playing of roles in life situations similar to the simulated one.

Notes

(i)   Tutors should be aware of the importance of eliciting comments from others. It is not part of a tutor's function to tell people what they should have done in the interaction nor what they should do in a life situation.

(ii) There are certain situations, however, when it would be appropriate for a tutor to tell people what they should have done during interaction but these are of a specific nature. For example, if the role-play is being used to teach procedure that has to be followed precisely, then and then only would it be part of the tutor's function to bring role-players to the point where they recognised that their procedure in the interaction was at fault.

(iii) Tutors who operate within a formal educational setting tend to be didactic and to dominate discussion, so it may be difficult for tutors with such inclinations to exercise the self-control necessary for effective work in the discussion stage of a role-play. 'What do you think happened'? a tutor may ask and when an answer is given he or she may well feel tempted to say, 'No, that's not right'. Such temptations need to be resisted. People take on roles in a simulated situation and are required to think and act for themselves in a dynamic encounter. Observers watch behaviour and come to their own understanding of what transpired. If role-players are to be brought to better role-performances this will come about only if they appreciate the weaknesses in their own behaviour and are then encouraged to try to effect improvement. Equally, if observers are to improve they also need to be encouraged to develop their own judgement and not to rely on the judgement of the tutor, no matter how experienced he or she may be.

(iv) Tutors should be sensitive to the feelings of those who were involved in the interaction. Few people like to be seen to be ineffective, and thus the giving of advice requires great care. It can be helpful to give a role-player opportunity to comment on his or her own work before eliciting comments from observers. (The tutor in Example A, which follows, adopts this procedure.)

ALTERNATIVE PROCEDURE

When describing the setting-up of an exercise it was stated that this was the responsibility of the tutor. However a tutor may choose to delegate this responsibility to a member (or members) of the tutorial group. In which case:

1. The tutor   (i) declares the educational theme
               (ii) asks a member to set up an exercise.
2. That person   (i) chooses the situation
               (ii) conducts the briefing
               (iii) allocates roles.

If members of the tutorial group are experienced the tutor may also delegate responsibility for leading during the discussion stage.

Notes

The tutor could be allocated a role. If he were, his behaviour during interaction would be subjected to comment in discussion along with that of the other role-players in the simulated situation.

If the tutor has delegated responsibility for leading the discussion he might choose to take part in the discussion but only on the same basis as the other members of the group.

   The tutor always reserves to himself the responsibility of ensuring that work undertaken is relevant and that no undue pressure is brought to bear upon role-players.

In the examples B and D below, the tutor adopts this alternative procedure.

TO SUM UP

The main duties and responsibilities of the tutor are:

(1) to determine educational objectives.
(2) to undertake necessary preparation.
(3) to set up exercise or to delegate this responsibility to others.
(4) to arrest temporarily or stop interaction when it seems necessary/desirable to do so.
(5) to encourage members of the group to comment on interaction.
(6) to help members put interaction into perspective.
(7) to encourage members to come to a realistic appreciation of present level of knowledge/competence.
(8) to encourage development of skills.

The following examples have been chosen to highlight specific aspects of role-play and to emphasize the different functions and responsibilities of the tutor.

EXAMPLE A.   This illustrates the different stages of a role-play exercise. The tutor has chosen the situation and conducts the briefing. Emphasis is placed upon the function of observers and upon the tutor's part in the discussion. In this example the tutor is operating in a formal educational setting.

EXAMPLE B.   In this example the choice of situation and therefore the conduct of the briefing are the responsibility of two members of the training group. The tutor is allocated a role in the interaction. There are no observers, and the information required before interaction begins is more detailed than in Example A.

EXAMPLE C.   Here role-play is being used with mature students and the focus of attention is upon the stopping of interaction by the tutor.

EXAMPLE D.   This highlights interaction. The tutor in this example operates in an informal setting and is using the technique to provide members of the group with the opportunity to look at their own work situation. The group chooses its own situation, allocates roles and conducts the briefing.

EXAMPLE E.   This does not focus upon one specific aspect of the organisation of a role-play but shows how the device can be used with a fairly large group.

EXAMPLE A

This example illustrates the different stages in a role-play exercise. It also illustrates the part the tutor plays in briefing and discussion when he or she, working in a formal educational setting, has selected the simulated situation on which the role-play is to be based.

A tutor is in action with a group of students, about twelve in number, in training for the teaching profession. The tutor, having decided to use role-play as the teaching method, is setting objectives.

TUTOR: We are going to look today at an aspect of a teacher's work that has little to do with the subject of teaching but much to do with pupil-management. I know that when you were out on teaching practice some of you had problems in this area. Someone said to me, 'How can I persuade pupils to work when they don't want to do so?' And I had no specific answer to give. No one can teach any of you how to manage pupils displaying uncooperative behaviour. Pupil-management skills you develop for yourselves. However, it is possible to alert you to certain principles and to give you an opportunity to discover guide-lines which each of you may then tuck away at the back of your mind to use when required.

BRIEFING

TUTOR: Here then is the situation.

A pupil in the second year of a comprehensive school is doing very poor work. This pupil came from the primary school with a very good record. In the first year work was good and there were no behavioural problems. This second year the story is different. As the year has progressed the pupil has become less and less interested in working and now, in the middle of Term Two, is seriously behind the majority of the class. The pupil appears to have lost interest, is troublesome in class, inattentive and often quite rude. The pupil is frequently late for school, takes the odd day off, and seems to have little physical energy. Matters came to a head last week when the pupil failed to hand in an exercise to be done at home. The teacher spoke to the pupil and asked that it should be handed in the next day. This did not happen. Three days later the exercise was handed in but when the teacher was correcting the work it became obvious that it was a direct copy of an exercise done by another pupil. The teacher did not hand the exercise back but asked the pupil to stay behind at 4 o'clock the day following and to tell her parents that she would be late.

That is the situation. There are two roles: Teacher and Pupil. Who will take these roles?

GLADYS: I'll do the teacher.

DORIS: And I'll be the pupil.

TUTOR: Good—Gladys, what do you teach?

GLADYS: French.

TUTOR: And how long have you been teaching?

GLADYS: This is my first job—I'm just out of college.

TUTOR: Gladys, make up your own mind whether or not you have already discussed the situation with your Head of Department in the interval between recognising the exercise was copied and asking the pupil to see you. Now we wouldn't know that, so keep that information to yourself. Doris, remember this is the second term of your second year and up until this year both at the primary school and in your first year you seemed to enjoy school and certainly your work was good. You will need to decide for

yourself what caused your change of situation. Again, we would not know that
so keep it to yourself. But what was it—Trouble at home? Feeling all right?
What's worrying you? What is it that is making you behave so
differently?—You decide. Anything anyone is not sure about?

GLADYS: Am I her class teacher as well as French teacher?

TUTOR: Would you like to have the dual function?

GLADYS: I don't think so. I'll just be the French teacher.

DORIS: Have I given trouble in other classes?

TUTOR: What do the rest of you think about that?

A STUDENT: There's been some talk in the staffroom about the pupil's behaviour this year but nothing serious.

TUTOR: Right—so there has been some general concern, Doris, about the
pupil's behaviour but nothing major until this happened. Gladys and
Doris, have you got enough information to make the situation credible?
You have? Good. Give yourself a moment or two to fill in your own
background, and do this independently. I'll have a word with observers.
Try to notice the effect the teacher's behaviour, verbal and non-verbal, has
upon the pupil and *vice versa*. Notice whether the teacher appears to be
trying to understand or to condemn. Pay special attention to the opening
stage—what does the teacher try to do first of all? At the conclusion of the
meeting notice how they part—attitude towards each other. Ask yourselves
what was accomplished.

(Briefing completed, Gladys arranged one part of the tutorial room as a classroom. Observers got themselves into positions where they could witness interaction and yet not distract either Gladys or Doris. Doris went out of the room.
When Gladys was ready the tutor went out of the room, told Doris that all was
ready, came back into the room and sat with observers. Doris, in the role of the
pupil, knocked on the door. The teacher called, 'Come in' and interaction began.)

INTERACTION

The pupil came into the room. She was asked to sit down and the teacher also
took a seat. Then the teacher began by asking the pupil why she had copied
another pupil's work. This the pupil denied. The teacher rose and fetched the
two exercises from her desk. She handed them to the pupil and asked her to
compare the work. Did she still deny that her exercise was a copy? The pupil
did. Faced with this the teacher switched to the late submission and the
pupil's poor general attitude to her work. She questioned the pupil on these
points but the pupil was not forthcoming. The teacher began to lose patience
and the pupil became more sulky. The situation ended with the teacher
dismissing the pupil and saying that unless her behaviour improved she, the
teacher, would have no option but to report her to the Head. The pupil left.

DISCUSSION

TUTOR: That was a very difficult problem to deal with, but Gladys, what do you think you accomplished?

GLADYS: Nothing.

TUTOR: Could you say why not?

GLADYS: I got off on the wrong foot and I think I put her back up at the start and I felt I was struggling from then on. I don't think I should have tackled her about the cheating at the beginning.

TUTOR: What do the rest of you think!

OBSERVER (1):   I think it was fair enough to explain to the pupil just why she had been asked to see you.

OBSERVER (2):   Yes, I agree, but not to tick her off.

TUTOR: To do what then?

OBSERVER (2):   To say what the problem was and then to try to find out why the pupil did what she did.

OBSERVER (3):   The teacher should try not to condemn if she is hoping to find out why the pupil's behaviour is so different this year.

TUTOR: Doris, did you get the impression that the teacher was trying to understand your position?

DORIS: Not really.

GLADYS: I didn't give Doris much time to talk—I was doing all the talking and not really noticing at first. Then, when I saw her getting more and more resentful I just did not know where to go so I said what I did.

TUTOR: It is difficult, isn't it, but somehow or other you must try to give the impression that you are concerned to understand.

OBSERVER: Perhaps if Gladys had given the pupil time to explain why she hadn't handed in her exercise that might have been better.

TUTOR: Would it necessarily?

GLADYS: No, I don't think it would because I might still have been trying to blame her. That really was my biggest mistake and that must have come across.

DORIS: It did.

TUTOR: What are some of the other issues that the teacher might have taken up?

OBSERVER: The pupil's lack of energy.

ANOTHER OBSERVER: Yes, and also the fact that she had done so well up to now.

DORIS: I would think it important to start from what is good rather than with what is bad.

TUTOR: These are good points you are making. Gladys, what would you wish to remember from this exercise?

GLADYS: To talk less and notice more. To give a pupil opportunity and time to explain and to try to see things from her point of view so that I didn't just blame her. I would hope that I wouldn't be so impatient but that might be difficult.

TUTOR: It is not always easy to be patient. Any other points that observers would like to make?

OBSERVER (4): It seems to me that if a pupil leaves your room disliking you more than she did when she came in you've accomplished nothing.

OBSERVER (5): But you can't just aim for liking from a pupil.

OBSERVER (4): I didn't say that. I meant that if a pupil goes out feeling that she had been unfairly treated she is going to be more resentful than she was when she came in, and the teacher then has only made matters worse instead of better.

TUTOR: Are you saying that maybe it could be sensible to overlook a present misdemeanour for a long term benefit?

OBSERVER (4): I don't think I went as far as that but I might be prepared to. I suppose it would all depend. . . .

GLADYS: On what?

OBSERVER (4): The circumstances. I think if you had really got to the bottom of the problem you could maybe show confidence in the pupil by overlooking the present misbehaviour in the hope of probable better behaviour.

TUTOR: That's an interesting comment because the outcome of such interviews may well depend upon the confidence each has in the other. Certainly if a pupil feels that a teacher is trying to understand difficulties the chances of her being cooperative are more likely. That role-play has highlighted important points for the conduct of disciplinary interviews. Perhaps the most crucial points for you to remember are:

(i) to give a pupil opportunity to state her own case.
(ii) to listen without judgement to what is being said.
(iii) to notice the accompanying non-verbal signals and from these to try to appreciate what the pupil can't or won't say in words.
(iv) to look below the surface for possible explanation of conduct.
(v) to encourage the pupil to get to the root of her own problem.
(vi) to be sensitive to the feelings of the pupil as a person.
(vii) to be prepared to take time to try to resolve the problem even if this requires a second meeting.

2

EXAMPLE B

Focus: Delegation of responsibilities for briefing and conduct of the Role-play.

In the context of training for Youth and Community Work, the tutor has asked two students, Adam and Jim, to select some aspect of work and to use role-play in illustration. This assignment has been given one week in advance of the training session.

TUTOR: Last week we looked at the different placements into which you will be going next term and we considered some of the situations that you might encounter. Jim and Adam were asked to select some particular aspect of work and to examine it through role-play. They have selected Public Relations.

ADAM: We believe that it is impossible to over-emphasise the importance of good public relations. We believe, also, that the relationship between the worker and members of the community is built up gradually through mutual awareness and understanding. We know that sometimes it can be exceedingly difficult to get on good terms with others and so we have chosen for our work today a situation that may well arouse strong feelings and therefore put us under considerable pressure. In the end we have to be able to control our own feelings and not to 'lose the heid' at the slightest provocation. We will give you roles and would ask you to play these strongly and positively and in a manner that will present us with problems. Here is our chosen situation.

BRIEFING

The warden of the XYZ Community Centre has received a notice signed by fifty persons resident near the centre opposing a known proposal that the opening hours of the centre should be extended to include late-night opening on Saturdays and normal opening hours on Sundays. The warden will be played by me and Jim will be the chairman of the management committee. I'll hand you over now to Jim who will give you further information.

JIM: I expect you have all studied the *Community Brief* which was distributed two days ago. This gives you all the necessary basic information on population, employment, incidence of truancy, facilities within the community etc. Is there any additional information that you would require?

JEAN: I see that Miletown is a quite small town but how near is it to a larger one?

JIM: Where will we place it? Twenty miles from a city? Agree? Let's take it then that there is a half-hour bus service to the city except on Sundays when it is an hourly service. The last bus leaves the city at 10.00 p.m. during the week and at 9.00 p.m. on Sundays.

Any other questions? No? Let's deal now with the Situation Brief—that is on the yellow page. You will have noted that the XYZ Centre has been opened for five years. The present hours are every day in the week except Sunday 10.30 a.m.–10.30 p.m. Late-night Friday until midnight. Sunday opening 2.00–6.00 p.m.

JIM: All categories of persons are catered for at the Centre and you will note that membership is fairly high in relation to population. The Centre, after a very sticky period at the beginning, now is held in pretty high regard. Please look now at the lay-out of the Centre. You will see that it is situated up a short drive and the nearest houses are a hundred yards off. Note, too, that the hall where discos etc. are held is at the back and furthest away from any dwelling houses. All right? Any questions?

(Certain questions were asked and additional information supplied.)

ADAM: We ask you to accept that when the petition was received by the warden he immediately got in touch with his chairman. They discussed the matter and felt that it should be put on the agenda for the next meeting of the management committee due to take place in a fortnight. Meantime the Warden acknowledged the letter containing the petition and stated that the matter would be given every consideration at the next meeting of the management committee. This meeting took place and it was decided that the warden and chairman should invite a representative group of the petitioners to meet them to discuss the problem. The interaction will be this meeting.

ALLOCATION OF ROLES

JIM: We have said that I will play the chairman and Adam the warden. Can we now allocate the other roles? You will see that we have listed these on the board and as you select your role we will put your name against it.

Senior citizen
A shift worker
Local councillor
Shopkeeper
District nurse
Head teacher of the comprehensive school
Two housewives
Bus conductress
Warden's secretary

We will give you fifteen minutes for your own briefing. We shall take it that you held two meetings at which those who signed the petition were present. The last one was held after the letter came inviting some of you to meet the warden and chairman and you were selected to represent the total group. Get all your facts and arguments. We ask that at least two of you be quite aggressive in approach and that whoever is your main spokesman/ woman should on a previous occasion have lodged a complaint with the warden about empty beer cans being thrown into his/her garden. Two other members of the group were disappointed that a local person was not appointed to the office of warden and both have as a consequence been critical of much that has been going on at the Centre.

If you wish any points clarified just ask. Would Rosemary who has put herself down to be the warden's secretary join us.

INTERACTION

Twenty minutes later the interaction begins, with the tutor playing the role of the shopkeeper. There are no observers.

EXAMPLE C

Focus: stopping of interaction;
Group: mature student social workers operating within a prescribed programme with a regular tutor;
Theme: leading a discussion group;
Objective: to use role-play to give students an opportunity to practise leading a discussion group.

TUTOR: Last week we were discussing the skills of the group worker and you made the point that, increasingly, the social worker is required to operate with groups. I know that you have all had considerable experience in the field as case workers but you admit to little experience when it comes to handling a group. Today, we will try to find out what's involved.

BRIEFING

TUTOR: I ask you to accept that you are social workers attending a conference. You have just had a plenary session on The Role of the Social Worker. You have been divided into small groups to discuss the professional status of today's social worker. At the end of your discussion you will be required to report back at the next plenary session. Clear? Jack, will you be the leader? Jim and Jean, will you please join me as observers? The rest of you will be members of the discussion group.

Each of you take a moment or two to make up your minds about your present attitude.

Remember we are concerned in the exercise with the work of the leader of a discussion group. Any questions?

MEMBER: Do we know each other?

TUTOR: Can we take it that you have worked together as a group at an earlier session under a different leader but you did not know each other prior to coming to the conference. All right?

Jack, when you think everyone is ready—begin.

INTERACTION

JACK: Well, ladies and gentlemen we have been asked to discuss the question of the professional status of the social worker. We are all here from different areas. We have different specialisms and interests and as we have been asked to report back to the parent group it would be interesting to hear your personal views. My own feeling in the matter is that with the new integrated service we are all working together with mutual respect and understanding of each other's ability and I feel that if we go forward together into the British Social Workers' Association we will stand a greater chance of. . . .

(Tutor breaks in and leads out into discussion.)

DISCUSSION

TUTOR: What is happening within the group?

OBSERVER A: They all appear to be listening to what the speaker is saying, but from facial expressions one or two at least have lost interest.

OBSERVER B: I felt the leader started off well. He outlined the task and asked for views, but then he went on to express his own.

GROUP MEMBER: Yes, that put me off.

OBSERVER A: This came across because you made a movement with your hand that suggested you were mildly irritated.

TUTOR: So there were signs of people beginning to be restive. Were you aware of these signs, Jack?

JACK: No. I wasn't looking for them. I felt cold and quite unsure of myself. I was tense.

OBSERVER B: You looked tense.

JACK: I felt so. I was concerned with my own problems. With one part of me I was speaking and with the other I was racing ahead wondering what I would say next.

TUTOR: Did anyone in the group appreciate that the leader was in some difficulty?

MEMBER: Yes, I did and I wanted to help. I was just waiting for an opportunity to do so.

TUTOR: I gave the group very little time to function but the leader did have the opportunity to bring members in. This he created for himself and then let it go by.

JACK: Yes. I asked for their views and didn't wait to hear them.

TUTOR: You would not have done that had you asked a client in a case work situation. Try to transfer the knowledge you have into this type of situation.

Incidentally why do you think leaders tend to rush on and let such an opportunity slip?

REPLIES: Keen to express their own views.

Silence can be frightening.

JACK: It is difficult to tolerate silence if you are not very sure of yourself.

TUTOR: You were flung in at the deep end and made your own error of judgement. Now take time to reflect upon what you have learned. Members re-establish your own positions within the group. We will go right back to the beginning. This is now the group discussion. When you are ready, Jack, begin.

Teaching points

In this example the tutor intervened before there was any vocal interchange. She chose to do so for the following reasons:

1. to draw the leader's attention to the non-verbal response of group members to his opening remarks.

2. to identify the learning points while the error of judgement was still fresh in memory.

3. to give the leader opportunity to acquire the information necessary for his own progress.

EXAMPLE D

(Some of this example is a transcription from an exercise, recorded with the permission of the participants.)

This illustrated a role-play that emerges out of a conversation. Although the tutor has had at the back of her mind the hope that she will be able to involve the young men in role-play this has been by no means certain.

Group: Young apprentices released from their firms to attend a residential course on the theme Relationships in Industry. The tutor was not known to the men prior to the training session and the technique of role-play was unfamiliar to them.

Objectives: to stimulate discussion on the course theme; to provide the apprentices with the opportunity to reflect upon their own relationships at work.

At the opening of the training session time is spent in conversation with the apprentices during which the tutor listens to what the men are saying as they describe the different circumstances within their own firms. At a suitable moment the tutor speaks.

TUTOR: You have been talking about relationships and you all seem to agree that there is often conflict between the older man and yourselves. What are some of the causes of the rows? Could you show me the sort of thing that happens?

The men then divide into small groups of five or six. There are three sub-groups. They discuss their own circumstances and each group set up its own role-play.

The Roles:

Willie	a tradesman
Jock	an older tradesman
Charlie	another tradesman
Bob	a young apprentice
Dave	the foreman

INTERACTION

Jock is working at his bench and Charlie and Bob are also working. Willie goes to Jock with a message from the foreman.

WILLIE: Jock, Dave wants you.

JOCK: Aye, wait a minute. I'm just comin'. (Jock puts his work down and goes away to see Dave. Bob comes in.)

BOB: Oi, seen Jock about?

CHARLIE: No, I never saw him.

BOB: Well, I'll just take a loan of his spanner. (He does and moves away. Jock comes back.)

JOCK: Anybody seen my spanner here?

CHARLIE: No.

JOCK: Who's got that spanner? I'm on bonus here—I'm no' makin' it. I bet that stupid laddie's got it. Here, you, Bob have you got that spanner o' mine?

BOB: Aye, I just took a loan of it. I didn't think ye'd be needin' it. You werena there. I was needin' it badly so I just took it.

JOCK: What do you mean, you were needin' it badly—don't you think I was needin' it?

BOB: I had to finish off this job so. . . .

JOCK: I'm no bothered—I'm on bonus here.

BOB: Dinna be so bad-tempered.

JOCK: What do you mean   ? How do you think *I'm* going to make my money if you. . . .

BOB: Oh, I just took a loan and I'll gie ye it back. It's no that I'm going to keep it or anything like that.

JOCK: I'm no bothered if you keep it. You came and took it without asking me. Can ye no buy one of yer own? I could have been lookin half the day.

BOB: Och, man, ye wouldna grudge me that. I've no money to buy a spanner. You ken that fine with the apprentice wage I've got.

JOCK: You make a fair wage. What do you think I had to work on when I was young?

BOB: Oh, here we go again, the old routine—when I was a boy!

JOCK: What do you mean, when I was a boy? You've got it good now, you've got it made.

BOB: Ach,   ! How do you expect me to live on the wages I get.

JOCK: Och, I'll get you the violins now.

BOB: When you were a boy all the tools an' that were cheap. It was about a penny to get into the pictures or something like that.

JOCK: Now, don't you get cheeky with me. I'm your elder remember.

BOB: Ach, elder ma foot, ye've one foot in the grave anyway. (The foreman enters and moves towards them, sensing trouble)

DAVE: Come on now, you two.

JOCK: You shut up. Who are you to butt in? This is between the laddie and me.

DAVE: Listen Jock. You're going out of the door if you don't cut this out.

JOCK: Oh, am I. . . .

TUTOR: (*Breaking in*) And we had better leave it there.

TUTOR: You were involved, weren't you? Would you really have gone for him?

JOCK: Yes, I think I would.

TUTOR: I was beginning to think I had a fight on my hands. (Turning to the others,) What did you think? Could the crisis have been avoided?

(Discussion followed then.)

TUTOR: Let us take the same situation again. Do you remember that we talked about seeing the other person's point of view? Well, try this time to show Bob and Jock reacting to each other in a more tolerant way. Now, Bob and Jock, don't turn yourselves into angels. You are the same people but this time prepared to give and take a little. All right?

The group takes a minute or so to agree at what point the situation would begin.

LEADER: This is the same situation and the scene begins when Jock comes back to his bench.

JOCK: Anyone seen my spanner lying around?

CHARLIE: No, I never saw it.

JOCK: Aw, who's got that spanner? I bet that stupid laddie's got it. Hey you, got my spanner there?

BOB: I've got it here, Jock. You werena there so I took a loan of it.

JOCK: I've got work to do, son.

BOB: I just took a wee loan of it. I didn't think you would miss it.

JOCK: Look, we're on tight times here. I'm on bonus. I'm hard put to make my money without you takin' my tools away.

BOB: Och, come on Jock—I just took a wee loan of it for a minute. I'll gie ye it back. You werena using it anyway.

JOCK: Right. Now look, if you're wanting my tools. . . .

TUTOR: We'll leave Jock and Bob to sort out that problem. But what about yourselves? How does your behaviour stand up in similar situations? Do you make an effort to understand the older men? Or do you expect them to do all the understanding?

There followed an interesting discussion.

Teaching points

The term role-play was never used.

The technique as such was not described.

The tutor, knowing nothing of the work situation from which the apprentices came, left choice of the simulated situation to them.

Each group conducted its own Briefing and gave the tutor and the other groups the essential background information prior to the Interaction.

Interesting consequences of these role-plays were the growth in self confidence of the young men, and their greater ease in relating to tutors on the course.

EXAMPLE E

(This role-play exercise was used with a group of thirtysix students taking a course on Speaking in Public. It illustrates procedure with a large group.)

The given situation outlined by Tutor

A public meeting has been called to consider the attitude of local residents to the proposed use of East Hall as a Residential Home for disturbed adolescents.

The given brief

East Hall is set in extensive grounds. It was originally a private dwelling house on the outskirts of Milend—a small country town.

During the Second World War the Hall was taken over as a military hospital and after the war it lay empty for some years but in 1955 it was bought and was run as a hotel. This enterprise did not prove to be financially rewarding and some ten months ago the Hall was again up for sale and was purchased by the regional council. Recently an article appeared in the local press to the effect that the council intended using the Hall as a residential home for disturbed adolescents. In terms of accommodation and facilities for recreation and sport, East Hall is ideally suited for this purpose.

This announcement came as a great surprise to the local residents. Letters have appeared in the Press both for and against the project. Public feeling is running high and nowhere is it stronger than in Northside Housing Estate. Milend is no longer a small town. It has grown considerably. As you will see from the map on the wall, East Hall is now within its boundaries. You will notice also that there is easy access from the Hall to Northside dwelling houses, Shopping and Recreational Centres.

The only information available from the regional council at the moment is that:

(1) Residents will be between the ages of fourteen and sixteen.
(2) It will be a co-educational establishment.
(3) All training will be undertaken by the appointed staff.
(4) Residents will not attend the local comprehensive school.
(5) Residents will come from a variety of backgrounds.
(6) All will be in need of remedial care.
(7) There will be approximately 25 pupils initially.

Roles

Chairman.
Local District Councillor who has agreed to attend and to speak.
Head Teacher of Northside Comprehensive School.
(These will form the platform party.)
Members of the community.

TUTOR: Are there volunteers forthcoming for the platform party? (Three
volunteered and roles are agreed.) Each of you now should do your own
Briefing. (to remainder of the group) So that we may have different
opinions expressed would members of the audience divide into three
categories:

(a) persons opposed to the project;
(b) persons supporting the project;
(c) persons at present neither strongly for nor against.

In addition each of you should choose a role, e.g. housewife and parent; senior
citizen; bus driver; postman; unemployed; school pupil; shopkeeper; manager
of community centre; teacher; nurse.

(*To Chairman*) You will require to discuss following points with the District
Councillor and the Head Teacher:

(a) speaking order;
(b) time allowed each;
(c) conduct of the open debate.

During briefing certain questions are asked, and answers are given by the
tutor. Briefing completed, the room is arranged as for a public meeting, the
platform party take up their positions, the chairman calls for order and the
meeting begins.

OBSERVATIONS

It should be noted that:

(i) the situation in each example quoted, had relevance for the particular
training group;
(ii) group members are given or assume roles that are reasonably familiar to
them;
(iii) briefing is sufficient to allow people to play their roles in the simulated
situation;
(iv) steps are taken to ensure that all appreciated what they are being asked to do;
(v) discussion followed interaction.

The effectiveness of role-play as a teaching tool is likely to be prejudiced if a
tutor is not aware of the importance of the above points.

In all probability readers will have realised that the tutor in each of the examples had no difficulty in persuading members to participate. This will not always be the case, even with experienced tutors.

As a training method role-play has no immediate attraction for the majority of people. Indeed, faced with the possibility of having to participate, most people usually advance reasons for non-involvement. These may stem from fear at the thought of having to perform in front of others or from scepticism about the method *per se*. Whatever the reason for reluctance to participate, it is the task of the tutor to try to allay fears and doubts at least sufficiently to persuade some members of the group to take part.

It is necessary, therefore, that some attention is paid to the validity of role-play as a learning device and to some of the obstacles to personal involvement. It is with these matters that the next section is concerned.

THE VALIDITY OF ROLE-PLAY AS A LEARNING TECHNIQUE

Role-play is a valid aid and is a device which can be used with benefit to those who are under instruction or for whom an adult has responsibility.

As soon as such a claim is made, questions and doubts form in the mind. Possibly the most frequently expressed misgivings are:

(1) a technique based on a 'let's pretend' principle is too childish for training purposes beyond primary school;

(2) the technique requires acting ability which many lack and therefore it would have only very limited appeal;

(3) a device based on performing in simulated situations is too artificial to be valuable;

(4) role-play invades the privacy of the individual and is a dangerous device to use in that it could lead to problems that the adult in charge might not be able to handle.

Certainly in some cases misgivings about role-play stem from misconception but it would have to be acknowledged that most people's doubts arise from their fear of manipulation and/or their questioning of the validity of role-play in an educational programme that has important objectives.

It is hoped, however, that if the validity of role-play is recognised it will be regarded in the same way as other training methods and—to be used or not to be used, according to circumstances.

Role-play is too personal and too dangerous to be regarded as a valid teaching tool.

Most who voice this opinion do so because they consider that to engage in role-play is an invasion of privacy and likely to induce an emotional atmosphere which is educationally undesirable and personally dangerous.

Any training method, any classroom interaction can be an invasion of privacy and can give rise to an emotional atmosphere that is harmful. Few would quarrel with that observation. Doubters, however, would probably go on to ask, 'Is there not really something inherent in the structure of role-play that sets it apart from other techniques and therefore makes it particularly risky to use as an educational tool?

The short answer to that is Yes. There is something in the structure of role-play that does set it apart from other methods of learning and makes the possibility of its being too personal and too dangerous more likely. So has the case against role-play now been proven? Not so. It is the case against inexpert and/or irresponsible tutors that needs to be prosecuted.

Let us look at the two main reasons why role-play is used. These are to develop skills in specific areas and to promote greater understanding of human behaviour. It is with the second of these functions that role-play has generally been associated. For most sceptics, role-play is equated with examination in public of personal problems: we will return to this, but first let us consider the use of role-play to develop skills.

Suppose an exercise is set to give participants opportunity to develop skills as, for instance, a demonstrator or a chairman of a committee: the role-play gives participants opportunity to recognise behaviour appropriate to the particular role and then to practise playing the role. The chances of this being harmful are negligible and only likely to arise if the tutor allows interaction or discussion to stray into areas that have no bearing upon the training issue. As a chairman of a committee in the playing of that role in life is not concerned to delve into the personal problems of the committee members so in a simulation exercise this would be as inappropriate. If, however, in such exercises, interaction does become too personal it will be because the tutor has failed to keep control of the situation rather than because there is a weakness in the device.

When role-play is used to promote greater understanding of inter-personal problems it can be extremely personal and unduly dangerous if any one of the following happens:

(1) It is regarded as a kind of goldfish-bowl technique with some people struggling inside in deliberately troubled waters while others watch their antics from without.

(2) It is used to examine problems that are outwith the professional competence and/or experience of the tutor.

(3) In the course of a role-play the tutor loses self control.

(4) The tutor allows interaction or discussion to develop to the point where participants are exposed to stress that they cannot or do not wish to cope with.

However, if tutors use role-play to help people come to terms with personal problems the device is not harmful provided that the tutor operates within his own professional competence and is sensitive to what is happening, particularly during the interaction and discussion stages. Certainly, responsibility to ensure that interaction does not become too personal or too dangerous again rests with tutors.

Of course, these are relative terms so what might be considered too personal and too dangerous for one group would not necessarily be so for another. There is something inherent in the structure of role-play which makes the method an exceedingly valuable one for the promotion of greater awareness of the human condition. In certain circumstances and with a particular group a tutor may choose to use role-play to involve members of the group in an experience which is designed to disturb.

There is an award-winning film from America entitled *The Eye of the Storm*. This film records the efforts of a young American teacher to give her eight-year-old pupils opportunity to experience for themselves the meaning of racial discrimination. Starting from the assassination of Martin Luther King, the teacher elicits from her pupils their attitude towards those who are black and together they talk about the position of the Negro in American society. 'Is it fair to judge a person on the colour of his skin?' asks the teacher and the children chorus 'No' in reply. Pupils agree that people are not all alike. For instance, some have blue eyes while others have brown. The teacher then says that she has blue eyes and so all the blue-eyed pupils are the superior ones.

That being established the first act of the teacher is to give the blue-eyed pupils collars made of soft material which they are required to place round the necks of the brown-eyed ones. The class seating is re-arranged so that the two groups are segregated and work begins.

The tone of voice which the teacher uses when addressing or referring to, the 'inferior' pupils is markedly different from that which she employs when talking to the 'superior' ones. In addition all the favourite tasks are undertaken by blue-eyed pupils and those that none like doing are given to the brown-eyes. If they presume to try to assert a right to be treated as equals the resultant behaviour of teacher and favoured pupils soon make them aware that they are not considered to be equal and therefore have no rights.

The next day, at the beginning of the class, the teacher announces that she made a mistake yesterday. It is not the blue-eyed pupils who are the superior ones but the brown-eyes. This news is received with great glee or with some puzzlement and apprehension as the case may be. Positions are reversed. All the restrictions previously placed on one set of pupils apply now to the other set. Humiliations and frustrations felt the day before are reflected in the attitude of the brown-eyes towards the blue-eyes and particularly so as they fasten collars round the necks of the new inferior ones.

Reactions from those who see this film will no doubt vary. Some will consider it indefensible that a teacher should involve pupils in such an exercise. Others may incline to the view that the end justified the means.

Certainly it is true that the children were disturbed. There were tears and yes, there was cruelty. Pupils and teacher went through an experience together which, in all probability, none enjoyed. However, feelings were engendered and perhaps the children, as a consequence, had a better understanding of what it must mean to be discriminated against.

The teacher in the film took a risk which she considered justifiable educationally in her own circumstances.

Because role-play calls for the translation of thought and feeling into action and the experiencing of the consequences of the reaction of others, it is a valuable learning agent and as *The Eye of the Storm* demonstrates, an exceedingly powerful one.

In the hands of the tutor who is aware of educational responsibilities, and of the capacity of participants to meet the demands of a given exercise, provided the tutor is watchful during interaction, role-play is neither too personal nor too dangerous as a teaching tool. Moreover it should be remembered that interaction may be stopped at any time. If a tutor feels that matters are beginning to get out of hand, this is the action that should be taken to protect participants.

Role-play is too childish to be accepted as a valid technique for older pupils and adults

For a start the words 'play' and 'playing' are suspect. These can be ambiguous words because of their connotation of triviality. Think of these statements: 'Work comes before play'; 'What is Johnny doing?', 'Oh, he's only playing.' They seem to imply that within the concept of play the element of work does not exist and that playing is something to be done when work is finished. However, think of: 'If you wish to improve your playing you will require to work at it,' or 'She is only playing at her work.' So it is possible to work at play and play at work! 'Playing' is commonly used: (*a*) to describe trivial behaviour; (*b*) to describe leisure time activity; (*c*) to describe any of these activities at a work level.

Mistakes occur when those outside an activity misjudge the level of serious intent of those who are engaged *in* the activity. Thus a mother can conclude that her son is engaged in some trivial activity when, in fact, he is involved in something of extreme importance to himself. Likewise the student considering the term 'role-play' may conclude that he is being invited to take part in some trivial activity and refrain from doing so.

There is a difference between the 'let's pretend' games of childhood and the adult device called 'role-play'.

Play in childhood

How important is playing in the lives of children? Are they only enjoying themselves or is there some more serious purpose? The use of play in childhood is too well known to spend much time recalling details. For the purpose of this argument it will be sufficient to give examples of the way in which children play, summarise main purposes and draw our own conclusions.

Children want to be grown-up. Ask a four-year-old his age and he will answer in quarters or relate it to his next birthday. 'I'm four and a quarter,' or I'll be five on my next birthday.' Often it must seem to the young child that the only possible way of living in peace is to be adult: adults can do as they please—no one tells *them* what to do. Children want to know everything, adults know everything, therefore being adult is desirable. When Jane busies herself sweeping, dusting and washing up, she is not amusing herself but imitating her mother. She is taking a step towards being like mummy and therefore becoming more efficient and more independent. This kind of imitative role-playing brings a sense of achievement to children, as they practise behaviour which they will require in the future.

An extension of this imitative play occurs when it is allied to the imagination of the child. Most children identify with favourite television or storybook characters, or the more mundane shop-keeper, nurse or teacher. Through this playing a child has the opportunity to try out behaviour that he has observed and to add to it from his own imagination. In so doing he is gaining in self-confidence, developing his ability to communicate his thoughts, building up a store of information for future use, and of course enjoying himself.

A child has many problems to work out. Much that adults do and say is puzzling. Often children do not understand the attitude of adults towards them. It is quite usual for a little girl, after being reprimanded by her mother, to re-enact the scene. The child will assume the role of mother, cast a doll in the role of herself, and in so doing try to solve the problem of her mother's behaviour towards her.

Children can and do assume several roles, changing from one to another quite frequently, and thus looking at a problem from different points of view. For example, a child can speak in the role of teacher and reply to himself in the role of the 'good' pupil one moment and the 'naughty' pupil the next. This kind of role-playing is often used by the lonely child for company, the very imaginative child for creative outlet, and the emotionally disturbed or insecure child for release.

As a child grows grows older, he becomes less self centred and more socially orientated. That is, he is no longer sufficient unto himself but wants to be with others. Those others begin to have some importance in his life. Through playing together, children learn to submerge their own interests in the interests of each other. A child learns to work with others because if he does not he will have no playmates. He wants to be liked and accepted by his friends, so he cooperates. This is socially necessary. If opportunity for playing together is denied children, then anti-social behaviour often develops. Play lays the foundation for good social relationships in later life.

Through play then, children

(a) develop communicative skills;
(b) practise activities required in later life;
(c) attempt to solve problems;
(d) find an outlet for energy, curiosity and imagination;
(e) find a safety valve for emotional disturbance;
(f) learn to cooperate with others;
(g) enjoy themselves.

Role-playing in childhood is not something that adults impose upon children to teach them lessons about life; it is something that children do of their own accord. It is all a glorious 'let's pretend', the children being oblivious of any educational benefit that may be accruing to them.

The conception of role-play under consideration is different from the childish activity in important respects:

(1) the technique is consciously and deliberately used for specific training purposes;
(2) activity is under the control, but not the direction, of the person in charge;
(3) it does not require people to use their imaginations to pretend that they are different human beings from themselves playing out real life scenes;
(4) it does ask of them that they assume certain positions in simulated situations and interact with others in associated positions;
(5) it does require people to consider their own and other people's behaviour in a responsible manner with the hope that insights gained may be reflected in life.

Role-play demands acting ability, which most lack: therefore it can have no majority appeal

This doubt is expressed when role-playing is equated in the speaker's mind with acting in the theatrical understanding of the word. In my experience, when the difference between the two activities is appreciated this particular doubt ceases to exist.

There are, in fact, not two types of acting to be considered but three:

(1) acting in everyday life
(2) acting in the Theatre
(3) acting in a role-play.

Acting in everyday life

As soon as two people meet, each gains an impression of the other. In the majority of such daily encounters, little if any attempt is made consciously to organise behaviour and display self to the best advantage. There are, however, occasions when individuals do make a conscious effort to create a specific impression. For instance, taking leave of a host and hostess after a dull evening spent in their home, guests will utter appreciative comments, 'Thank you so much. We have had a lovely evening'. Guests 'act the part' of people who have enjoyed themselves. This is expected of them. Some people, of course, put on a better performance than others. Or take another example, this time from within the family. Father is ill. The children are anxious and tearful and mother, very worried herself, puts on a performance in front of the children, hoping that by so doing she will convince them that there is no reason for them to worry. There are a number of occasions when an attempt is made to create an impression which is not entirely a 'true' one. Particularly in the early years of adolescence the young find themselves in situations about which they have little information. From feelings of insecurity they often act in a manner calculated to boost their confidence. The apparently boorish fifteen-year-old may be putting up a front to hide his inner feelings. It can happen too if this behaviour is challenged by adults: an even more extreme performance is given.

The human being, then, is a social animal who finds it necessary for a variety of reasons to put on a performance and on occasions to create impressions that are perhaps not consistent with inner feelings. In this sense 'acting' is a natural activity with which all are familiar and at which most have a measure of skill.

Both theatrical acting and role-playing formalise the natural activity of acting for specific purposes. In both activities a number of people involve themselves in a social situation. This situation is contrived and the people in the situation do not behave exactly as they would in real life.

Starting from these similarities the activities of acting and role-play branch out in different directions.

Acting

Part of the behaviour that goes with the position of Actor is an apparent loss of identity and the assumption of a new identity for a period of time. The identity change is the part the actor plays or, in theatrical parlance, his role. (It could then be said that in his social role of actor, the actor plays many roles.)

In the course of his work an actor identifies himself with a particular character and those who watch him at work take him to be that particular person. For instance, the actor, the man, takes on the identity of Hamlet. Hamlet comes to life and goes through a pattern of behaviour during which he plays certain social roles. He is son to Gertrude, step-son to Claudius, friend to Horatio and Prince to the people of Denmark. It is the convention of the theatre that all who see this behaviour believe that it is the man Hamlet who is in action and not the actor in his own person. At the end of the performance Hamlet dies and the curtain falls. When the curtain rises again the live actor is applauded. He is himself again.

An actor is successful only in so far as he is able to involve the members of the audience in the experiences of the play.

Role-play

For those taking part in role-play there is no loss of identity. People are asked to become occupants of particular positions in certain simulated social situations. For instance, John is a student but for the purpose of role-play he assumes the role of teacher and in the simulated situation he behaves in the manner of a teacher. It is John Smith playing the role of teacher and he is free to play that role as he thinks it should be played. Those who watch him are interested in teacher-behaviour. His acting becomes a visual aid pin-pointing aspects of a teacher's work and drawing attention to them. As soon as these particular purposes have been served John stops acting as a teacher, then as a student he takes part in discussion.

During a role-play exercise those who have been acting out a particular situation can be imagined as saying, 'From the knowledge I possess at this moment I think the role would be played in this way.' In the subsequent discussion these conceptions of the role would be discussed, and so the function of those witnessing a role-play is different from that of people in a theatrical audience.

To sum up: the function of acting is to provide an audience with an experience that stimulates imagination and touches heart and mind. The actor is successful only so far as he is able to facilitate this imaginative experience for the individuals who make up the audience. They, in turn, communicate their response to the actor so that those who initiate experience and those who respond to it together build a performance.

The function of role-play is to provide an opportunity for discovering more about human behaviour and for acquiring the kind of information that will help people cope more effectively with their own relationships. The acting out of a situation is independent of audience reaction. The acting is the interaction between all those who are involved in the simulated situation. If there are people watching this interaction they observe what is happening while remaining detached from it.

An academic discussion on the distinction between acting and role-play can be exceedingly interesting. One can tease the mind with endless questions which often instead of clarifying the issue merely confuse. In practice, however, the problem almost solves itself. As one uses the technique of role-play and understands its purpose the difference between the two activities becomes obvious. Participants recognise that what is required is life-acting not stage-acting.

A device based on performing in simulated situations is too artificial to be valuable

This is probably the most frequently expressed misgiving concerning role-play and the biggest stumbling block to its acceptance.

That artificialities do exist in role-play is undeniable and yet, in spite of the contrived nature of the device, it can have potential as a teaching tool. Equally undeniable however, is that individuals can and do find role-play too artificial to be useful. It is not, therefore, my intention to deny the contrived nature of role-play nor to suggest that persons who do not see its potential lack perception.

My aim here is to try to identify the false and the true in a role-play exercise and to consider their relative importance. By doing so I hope that tutors will be in a better position to cope with the problem of artificiality if and when it is presented to them.

Real life situation

In a real situation at least two persons engage with each other in a particular setting and for some purpose. The encounter may be a chance meeting, in the street perhaps, and last no longer than it takes the persons to pass the time of day with each other. On the other hand, the meeting may have been pre-arranged (and not necessarily by those involved in the meeting): it may be of extreme importance and last for a considerable period of time.

Such encounters occur in the normal course of living and, unless a confidence trick is being perpetrated, everything and everyone is as it or they seem to be. For instance, if A goes into a shop to buy some fish, has an argument with the shopkeeper and leaves without buying anything—all that in fact is happening in the lives of the customer and the shopkeeper.

The different relevant elements in a real situation can now be identified. They are:

(1) setting in which the encounter takes place
(2) persons involved in the interaction
(3) purpose of the encounter
(4) effect that each person has upon the other
(5) give and take behaviour that occurs.

Simulated situation

It has been noted that a real situation occurs in the normal course of living and if we look at a simulated situation we will discover that it also occurs in the lives of the persons involved in it. Take an example.

In real life students and tutor meet in the context of a particular training session. Within this true situation another situation is consciously and deliberately invented, and in that world within a world people interact. Those who do interact in the contrived situation have been translated from their real or true role of student to the false role they have been asked to play. Those who watch the interaction remain in the real world of the training group, and role-players at the conclusion of the interaction come back into reality for the discussion.

The false elements in simulated situations are, therefore:

(1) setting in which the encounter takes place
(2) positions which are assumed
(3) information concerning

    (a) these positions
    (b) purpose of the encounter
    (c) events that lead up to the encounter
    (d) individual case histories;

and the true ones:

(1) effect that persons have upon each other
(2) give-and-take behaviour that occurs.

If we look again at that analysis we see that in both real-life and simulated situations people act on their own initiative in dynamic circumstances. Their behaviour is true in the sense that it actually happens. But let us re-examine the words false and true in the context of role-play.

The false elements in a simulated situation are certainly artificial, that is false in the sense that they are not as they seem but—and this is a very important point—not false in the sense of deceitful. In role-play there is no conscious attempt to pretend that the simulated situation is anything other than an invention. By common consent a situation is taken for the time-being to be a true one.

It was said that the interaction that occurs in simulated situations is true in the sense that persons actually do engage in give-and-take behaviour and have an effect upon each other. But in another sense this behaviour could be taken to be false in that it could be unlike anything that people had experienced in real-life. For example, in a training situation A was asked to take on the role of social worker and B that of client in a simulated interview. During interaction B's playing of the client role was so unlike anything that A had come across in life that she voiced the opinion that B's behaviour was false. Some observers took the same view. However, had A found that B's behaviour matched up to her real-life experience she might well have said, 'It was true to life', and observers might have agreed.

In whatever sense the words true and false are being used the problem of artificiality has to be resolved, and by each individual person.

So far as this misgiving is concerned it seems that the acceptance of role-play hinges upon:

(1) the relative importance individuals attach to the artificially contrived elements in a simulated situation;
(2) the extent to which individuals are seeking to equate behaviour in simulated situations with what they consider would happen in life.

In time most doubters come to appreciate that artificialities are necessary for the creation of the context in which interaction occurs and that role-play provides opportunity for learning, not mimicking.

Not all, however, will then go on to accept role-play as a valuable teaching tool. Some will but others will not. For the latter, role-play will remain too artificial for their use.

We have tried to examine some misgivings and misconceptions so that the technique might be better understood and perhaps recognised as a method of teaching that has validity. There is, of course, no guarantee that lessons learned through role-play will be carried forward and affect behaviour in real life but then no teaching method can guarantee success. Few would quarrel with the idea contained in the phrase 'horses for courses' and thus persons with educational responsibility for a particular lesson will try to choose the most effective method for the work to be covered. It is, therefore, as important to appreciate when role-play would not be an appropriate device as it is to recognise when it might be useful.

Undoubtedly, the first experience that a person has of role-play is likely to influence his or her attitude towards it and so it is important that tutors intending to use role-play with persons unaccustomed to the device should choose a way of introducing it that will minimise difficulties. It is to this matter that we now turn our attention.

PART ONE : SECTION THREE

METHODS OF INTRODUCING ROLE-PLAY TO PERSONS UNFAMILIAR WITH THE DEVICE

When introducing role-play to persons unfamiliar with the device, tutors are advised to base choice upon an assessment of what would be the most productive method having regard to personnel, educational objectives and circumstances in which the tutorial session will take place. In an effort to highlight the importance of suiting method to occasion, different groups and circumstances have been chosen in illustration and will be considered under three headings.

i *Training conferences and courses (p.46)*

Part time Youth Leaders attending a residential training conference.
Teachers attending a vacation course.
Pupils released from school attending a one-day school leavers' conference.

In the above examples the tutor's remit is for one session only and he or she has had no previous experience of working with any of the groups.

ii *School or college setting (p.58)*

Pupils in school
Students in college.
In both cases the tutor is taken to be working with a class that he or she meets regularly.

iii *Social settings (p.63)*

In the following examples the person who is using role-play does so in circumstances that are not explicitly educational:

A personal problem
A common problem.

45

i TRAINING CONFERENCES AND COURSES

FIRST EXAMPLE

Remit: To introduce role-play to a group of youth leaders attending a training conference.

Objectives: To give conference members opportunity to:

     (i) participate in role-play

     (ii) appreciate how an exercise is organised

     (iii) consider application of role-play in the context of their own work.

If such a remit has been given, what steps might be taken in preparation for, and in the undertaking of, the task?

Step 1. Collect from the organisers of the conference as much information as is necessary to provide a picture of: (*a*) Overall objectives of the conference; (*b*) how the session fits in to the pattern; (*c*) the persons to be involved.

Step 2. Consider implications of the information received.

Step 3. Reach decisions.

Step 4. Implement decisions at the conference.

Step 5. De-briefing.

These in outline are the steps that might be taken. Now, through example, let us consider the steps in detail.

STEP ONE: Collect Information

Suppose that the following information has been elicited:

(1)	Total number of persons	36: 24 men and 12 women
	Age range	17–45+
	Experience	Members drawn from Church Fellowships, Scouts and Guides; Boys' Brigade, local authority clubs and community centres.
	Occupations	Variety of occupations represented including students, clergy, teachers.
(2)		Conference organisers had included role-play in their programme following a request from some of the youth leaders.
(3)		Conference programme showed that the role-play session was due to take place on the second day from 2.00 p.m. until 4.00 p.m.

(4) In the morning sessions on that day were a lecture followed by group discussion, on the theme Leadership.

The implications of this information may now be considered.

STEP TWO: Consider Implications

(1) 36 is a fairly large group. It would be wise, therefore, to choose a method of introducing role-play that will involve everyone in the interaction.

(2) The wide age-range and the variety of occupations represented may present some problems. There could be a tendency for the experienced persons to dominate. This must be avoided as much as possible.

(3) The session is on the second day so the group should have settled in and members should know each other reasonably well. At least the strangeness of the first day will have gone. This is likely to be an advantage.

(4) Role-play was requested by some leaders so there must be some interest around.

(5) In all probability some members will have come across the device before but some may have had a poor experience of it.

(6) There is likely to be a high level of skill within the group.

STEP THREE: Reach Decisions

The following are possible:

(1) Proceed to a practical demonstration of role-play as soon as possible, and therefore keep introductory comments to a minimum. During these first few minutes, lay stress on members' interest in learning more about a training method, and try to create the impression that role-play is one of several teaching tools.

(2) Use the buzz group method of introduction as this will involve everyone in action simultaneously but in small units of three persons talking together. (Such small units are often called buzz groups presumably because the noise made by small groups comes across as a general hum or buzz.)

(3)   Thereafter, call for volunteers to help with a demonstration of the role-play sequence and try to show how a situation is translated into a role-play exercise.

(4)   Encourage remaining members to observe and comment on Interaction.

(5)   Then sub-divide main group—(trying to avoid any existing sub-groups in case in earlier sessions certain members were beginning to dominate).

(6)   Give a situation to each sub-group—this to be an uncomplicated one well within the experience of all.

(7)   Following sub-group sessions, re-unite for reports and questions.

(8)   Give out prepared handout covering objectives and organisation of role-play and including ideas for role-play exercise.

Possible timetable:	Introductory comments	5 minutes
	Buzz groups	15 minutes
	Demonstration	20 minutes
	Role-play in sub-groups	60 minutes
	Plenary session	20 minutes

Suggested buzz-group situation

A young person aged thirteen arrived home from an outing exhausted and some three hours after the expected time of 8.00 p.m. The parents had become increasingly worried as time went by. When their child eventually arrived home just after 11.00 p.m. they were very worried. On questioning their child they learned that the hill walk had turned out to be much more difficult than had been estimated by the person in charge of the outing. Some of those who had gone on the walk, including the child, had found the going very hard indeed. One of the parents telephoned the leader of the organisation that had sponsored the outing but that person had no knowledge of the late arrival home of the party. The leader, however, agreed to contact the assistant who had been in charge and suggested that the three meet to discuss the matter. A time was arranged.

Suggested sub-group situation

Six members of a particular youth club are sitting chatting in a small room. They have been there for fifteen minutes. Into the room comes the chairman of a particular committee who says that the room has been booked for a committee meeting. This person is annoyed when he/she finds that the room is already occupied.

The people in the room are asked to leave but they refuse to do so saying that there was no indication that the room had been booked and that they have as much right to be there as anyone else.

Task:
>> to consider the different options open to the chairperson;
>> to decide one course of action;
>> to take this action in a role-play.

Additional information:
>> Booking procedure—anyone wishing to reserve a room does so in the Office. Thereafter, a card is slipped into the holder on the door stating for whom the room has been reserved and between which hours. In this case, there was no card in the holder.

STEP FOUR: Implement Decisions

If at all possible arrive in advance of the session and make informal contact with as many of the conference members as possible. This will help the tutor to get the feel of the group and will give others an opportunity to size up the tutor. Then proceed as follows.

(1) Talk briefly to the conference, trying to establish an appropriate working atmosphere and to maximise participants' desire to become involved.
      Avoid any suggestion that role-play is a prerequisite for the success of the training programme.

(2) State the remit and outline the pattern of the whole session.

(3) Ask people to turn chairs round, making themselves into independent groups, each of three persons.

(4) Let them name each other A, B, C.

(5) Read out the prepared situation and ask that each buzz group determine the following additional information:
      The particular organisation that sponsored the hill walk (Scouts—Community Centre? or what?)
      The position of the one who had been in charge of the walk (Was the person a senior member—an assistant leader?)

(6) Give this additional information to all buzz groups: In each group A is the parent, B is the leader of the chosen organisation, C is the one who was in charge of the walk.
      The situation is that the Parent, the Leader and the Walk Organiser meet to discuss the situation of the late arrival home from the expedition in the light of the complaint by the parent.

(7) Answer any questions and then ask all buzz groups to have that meeting.

(8) Allow the role-play to continue—all buzz groups operating simultaneously—and after about five minutes stop proceedings. Re-allocate roles. As to Bs, Bs to Cs, and Cs to As.

(9) Brief groups. Each has a new role, being asked now to look at the problem from a different position. Disregard what has just happened. Imagine that this is still the meeting between the three persons.

(10) Allow second role-play to proceed for about four minutes. Stop and ask people to make the final switch and, when ready, to start the meeting which again is taken to be the original one.

It may well be that in the first round of role-plays some buzz groups are not involved and there is a fair amount of hilarity from them. The second time round there may be greater involvement and less hilarity and by the third time it could be that almost all the buzz groups appear to be working well in the simulated situation.

(11) Call for volunteers to help with a demonstration of role-play. Choose a situation likely to maximise interest (suggestions follow) and using these volunteers go through the different stages of role-play, paying particular attention to the work of the tutor, especially in Briefing. During the role-play it is advisable to stop interaction once or twice and to elicit observations on interaction from conference members e.g. What are you noticing? What's happening now?

(12) Answer any urgent questions at end of demonstration but proceed to next aspect of the programme as soon as possible.

(13) Divide the group into four or five sub-groups. Give to each group the chosen situation (i.e. the booking of the room). Ask each group to appoint a tutor and then to proceed to the role-play.

(14) Go round the groups making sure that all have understood what is being asked of them. Suggest to groups that if they finish the given situation they might like to devise another one for themselves.

(15) After the allotted time the groups re-assemble.

(16) Listen to what the different groups have to say. Encourage them to declare difficulties. Answer any questions and give help for future application of role-play.

(17) Issue prepared handout: this should include summary of main points covered in the training session, and ideas for role-plays.

STEP-FIVE: De-briefing

Think over the various steps taken in preparation and in performance and try to identify areas that were not as well handled as they might have been. Note these carefully for future reference.

Ideas for situations

1. Three weeks ago a notice was placed on the Youth Club noticeboard inviting members to sign up for a rock-climbing expedition. Twelve people signed up. A week before the date of the expedition the member of staff who posted the notice informed the Leader of the Youth Club that he was now unable to take the group away.

   The leader calls a meeting of the staff to try to resolve the situation in a way that will ensure that the twelve members are not disappointed.

2. John is sixteen. He is not bright. With people of his own age he is at a loss. He had attached himself to the Junior Club and is causing trouble. The warden of the community centre has received a letter of complaint from the parent of one of the young boys. In it the mother states that John has been bullying her son. In charge of the Junior Club is one of the part-time leaders.

3. It has been suggested that the town should promote a Summer Festival. There has been a reasonably enthusiastic response to the idea. Certain people have been invited to attend a meeting at which the suggestion will be considered in some detail. Members attending include representatives from the different youth organisations.

4. A bus was hired to take members of the Centre to a Ten Pin Bowling Alley. It is a rule that no drink is taken on to the bus. Two days after the outing the leader of the particular organisation that hired the bus received a letter from the hirers complaining of the damage done to the bus by some members of the party. Also enclosed was a bill for the amount of the damage to the bus. The leader decides to see the person in charge of the outing.

5. The leader of a particular organisation requires a certain amount of money to subsidize a project that he/she has in mind. The decision whether or not any assistance will be given rests with the Finance Committee. The leader puts his proposition to a meeting of this committee.

6. The leader has been asked by the organiser of a particular project if he/she could supply some volunteers for the project. The leader appreciates that the timing and nature of the project may make the task of seeking volunteers difficult. However, he/she calls a meeting of members and puts the request to them.

7. Feedback is required by the training section of H.Q. on the area of responsibility given to patrol leaders. A meeting has been called by the trainers in the division for commissioners and unit leaders to discuss the relationship of patrol leaders with their patrols.

8. This particular community centre organises weekly staff training sessions. Members of staff are encouraged to suggest matters for consideration and in particular to bring to the notice of the staff group any problems that have been encountered. One member brings forward the problem she has been having with a mixed group of young people. The group were working together very well until two people joined it, then the atmosphere seemed to change and where there used to be harmony now there is disagreement. At the last meeting a serious row developed between members.

9. Over a period of time the local press has given young people in the neighbourhood what many consider to be bad publicity. The good that they do in the community is ignored but any activity that could be described as anti-social is likely to be reported. Matters came to a head when an incident that occurred at the end of a Disco was reported in a highly sensational manner. A meeting of parents and youth workers has been called to discuss the matter.

10. An influx of young people from a new housing area has caused some disquiet in the Centre. At the Friday night Disco drink was brought into the Centre. Fighting broke out among certain members and the police had to be brought in to restore order. The incident caused members of the management committee to re-consider their attitude towards membership. Pressure is being brought to bear upon the committee from some parents. At a management committee meeting the issue is discussed.

11. In the opinion of some members of the committee of a youth organisation insufficient attention is being paid to the increasing number of immigrants within the community. At a meeting, ideas for the establishment of improved relationships are advanced.

12. A meeting of leaders of different organisations has been called for the purpose of selecting two who will represent the area at a national conference.

SECOND EXAMPLE

Remit	To introduce role-play to teachers attending a vacation course.
Objectives	To explain the organisation of role-play sequence. To consider the function of the tutor in the different stages.
Time	2 hours.

PREPARATION
Check on numbers
Consider available facilities and equipment

Reflect upon possible responses to participation in a role-play
Select method of introduction
Plan total programme.

Nature of group

It can be assumed that all members of this group will be skilled in teaching methods and will quickly appreciate the organisation of a role-play sequence.

It is probable that some teachers in the group may question the usefulness of role-play in the context of their own circumstances.

It is probable also that teachers may find it quite difficult to operate in the style of tutoring required in role-play, a style more democratic than that to which they are accustomed.

Selecting method

Suppose there are to be 20–25 teachers on the course. Several methods may be used for such a group. For instance:

(1) Demonstration of role-play by chosen helpers from outwith the group of teachers
(2) Tape-recording of a role-play
(3) A film or video-tape of a role-play.

Any one of these methods will demonstrate the technique in a satisfactory manner and will give the teachers an opportunity to recognise how role-play can be organised. Later, in discussion of what has been seen, there should be a profitable session on the usefulness of the device in the context of the classroom.

If, however, it is considered desirable to involve teachers in a role-play prior to any critical examination of merits and demerits, then some other method of introducing the technique should be tried.

It is sound educational principle to begin with the familiar and proceed to the unfamiliar. The method now to be outlined involves teachers in discussion—with which they are familiar before asking them to engage in a role-play—with which they are not familiar.

WHAT TUTOR SHOULD DO

(1) introduce him/herself; state nature of remit; declare objectives.
(2) Divide the large group into four sub-groups —A, B, C, D.
(3) Give same problem to groups A and B and, possibly a different one to groups C & D.

3

(4)   Ask each group to discuss its given problem and to list possible courses
        of action that might be taken to try to resolve the problem and to
        indicate the preferred course of action.

Example of type of problem envisaged. Note, it is not a classroom problem.
At this stage it is probably advisable that it should not be.

There has recently been considerable anger over the failure of the appropriate authority to have a pedestrian crossing at a very busy part of the High
Street. There are two crossings at either end of the street but these are 300
yards apart. The street is wide and straight and traffic is fast moving, having
just emerged from a much narrower street into a broader one. Accidents have
occurred and the latest one involved a young child.

Letters have appeared in the local paper but no action has been taken. The
group is made up of citizens who live in the area and who have met together to
consider what steps should be taken to resolve the present position. There has
been talk of routing traffic from King Street round into Green Street which is a
relatively quiet street for shoppers and thus making High Street safer.

 (5)   Read out the problem for A and B. Issue copies to the groups. Deal
        similarly with C and D.
 (6)   Ask groups to begin their task.
 (7)   Go round the groups answering any questions. If additional informa-
        tion is required by Group A for instance, the same information must be
        given to Group B.
 (8)   Give necessary time for discussion. People may need to be hurried
        along to reach decisions. Encourage them to make up their minds.
 (9)   Gather in lists.   .
(10)   Read out again A/B problem and the course of action that As have
        preferred.
(11)   Suppose that this has been to conduct a survey of shopkeepers in the
        area to ascertain degree of support for a by-pass. Ask Group A to choose
        an interviewer from their midst and Group B to select a shopkeeper to
        be interviewed. Let the shopkeeper indicate nature of shop.
(12)   Roleplay this interview.
(13)   A course of action from Group B's list is selected and if this is that three
        persons should visit the local councillor then Group B should provide
        the delegation and Group A the councillor.
(14)   Groups C and D are treated similarly and either they are taken after A
        and B have completed their two role-plays or they proceed concur-
        rently.
(15)   At the conclusion of the whole exercise it is important to go over the
        organisation of role-play, stressing the function of the tutor in all three
        stages. Try to avoid getting too deeply involved in an academic
        discussion on the validity of role-play. It is better to delay such

discussion until the teachers have an opportunity to experience for themselves whether or not the device attracts them as an educational tool.

FOLLOW-UP

The work just described will probably take about one hour. The aim, now, is to set up role-play exercises. It is important to help the teachers to appreciate that in a role-play people are being asked to think for themselves and to act on their own initiative. Therefore it is totally irrelevant for any person watching interaction to say, in effect, 'I wouldn't have done it that way', or 'You were quite wrong when you said that. . . .'

The following exercise would give teachers an opportunity to reflect upon their own capacity to refrain from dominating discussion either by advancing their own ideas or by making judgements on the views of others.

(1) Sub-divide groups into three units.
(2) Ask people to number off round their own unit.
(3) To avoid the problem of waiting for people to volunteer, pick a number at random e.g. 5. Number five in each unit is the teacher.
(4) Pick two other numbers, for example 1 and 3. The ones and threes are observers.
(5) Remainder of persons are members of the fifth form.
(6) Give out the situation:
     In this particular school the Form Teacher meets regularly with a group of Fifth Formers who are particularly interested in Current Affairs. Each week an issue that has hit the headlines is discussed. Sometimes the teacher states what the issue will be and at other times this is determined by pupils.
(7) Ask each unit from what is currently of interest to agree on the topic to be discussed.
(8) Advise the pupils that they do not necessarily need to try to be the most awkward in terms of behaviour. It is taken for granted that all within the group enjoy the regular meetings.
(9) While the units are conducting their own Briefing, talk to the observers and ask them to notice:
     the extent to which the teacher dominates proceedings;
     capacity to encourage comments;
     capacity to remain silent, etc.
(10) Allow role-play to begin.
(11) Stop interaction when you consider it appropriate to do so.
(12) Ask all members of each unit including observers to discuss Interaction among themselves.

The session should probably be concluded with a general discussion at which people may have questions answered either by the tutor or preferably by other people within the group.

Give out Notes on Role-play.

THIRD EXAMPLE

Remit   Pupils attending a one-day school leavers' conference, to be responsible for a session entitled Relationships at Work

Objectives   to introduce pupils to role-play;

to encourage them to observe inter-personal behaviour;

to provide opportunity for pupils to consider difficulties through role-play;

to stimulate discussion on adjustment to work relationships.

Unlike the previous examples, the main emphasis in this remit will not be on the device as such but upon its use as a visual aid in order to identify problems and to promote greater understanding of necessary adjustments.

Consequently, it is desirable that conference members should see the technique in effective and efficient use. So that this may happen the tutor should seek the help of persons able and willing to make up a tutorial team. Some time prior to the conference the tutor should meet with helpers to make the necessary preparation. At this meeting:

(1) The tutor relays basic information acquired from the conference organisers: numbers, ages, ability range, etc.

(2) The tutor and team then:

(*a*) determine learning points that the role-play demonstration will try to make;

(*b*) devise a suitable situation;

(*c*) allocate the roles within the situation to members of the team;

(*d*) discuss the briefing of conference members for their part as observers;

(*e*) consider follow-up work.

Suppose that the decisions taken at this meeting are that:

(1) The tutor is to make the introductory comments explaining purpose of session.

(2) The tutor is also to set up the demonstration role-play and brief the observers.

(3) The simulated situation is to be: First day at work in which the new member of the firm meets, first of all, his employer and secondly some of the people with whom he will be working.

(4)   In the demonstration the person taking on the role of the new employee is to display some rather awkward behaviour. This to be realistic and not in any sense exaggerated. The person taking on the role of employer to be brisk, efficient, but welcoming.

(5)   Immediately after the demonstration, conference members are to be given time to record their own observation.

(6)   The total group is to break up into smaller units with a member of the tutorial team in each group.

(7)   There will be discussion by members about their observations.

(8)   The tutor in each group will ask each member to list on paper some of his/her anticipated worries concerning future employment.

(9)   From their own lists the tutor and the group will select one that could be considered further, through role-play.

(10) Members are to be encouraged to observe and comment, the emphasis being on learning from each other.

When working with a group of this nature it is important that preparation for the role-play is thorough and that behaviour in the interaction is as was agreed. To think up a role-play at the last moment might prejudice the entire session and if interactants are not fully aware of objectives and perhaps more interested in displaying their own abilities this may give a concept of role-play that was not intended.

The demonstration should be introduced in a calm atmosphere that is conducive to learning. If school leavers are excited their tendency will be to look on role-play more in the nature of a theatrical performance. Through introductory comments and during the briefing, the tutor should try to encourage members to direct their attention towards educational objectives.

The tutorial team should regard school leavers at the conference as young adults. The area of concern is future work-behaviour and not present school-behaviour. Thus it is important that all should be thinking in terms of a work environment: this is likely to be facilitated by the manner in which the tutor speaks to the conference at the outset.

The simulated situation of the demonstration role-play should be sufficiently like a real work situation for it to be plausible. Members of the tutorial team need to have sufficient knowledge and experience of work situations to be able to role-play realistically and deal effectively with queries, etc., in the small group sessions.

If at all possible, there should be a de-briefing meeting at which members of the tutorial team evaluate work that has been done.

ii SCHOOL OR COLLEGE SETTING

In each of the previous examples the tutor is taken to be working with unknown groups and undertaking a one-off assignment.

The next two examples describe, firstly, how a subject teacher in a class room might introduce role-play into the learning programme and, secondly, how this might happen with students in the context of professional training.

In such circumstances the tutor will have greater knowledge of the group with whom he or she will be working, and therefore choice of method is bound to be less speculative. But it can happen, and particularly with students, that reaction to the device is more hostile than would be the case with unknown groups.

SCHOOL SETTING: Commercial Studies. Girls aged 15

The tutor in this example is assumed to be the subject teacher and to have decided to use role-play to help pupils prepare for their future work. The girls are all due to leave school at the end of the current session. The tutor has decided to involve pupils in role-play without labelling the device or describing it beforehand.

STAGE ONE

(1) Establish difference between work in school and work in an office.
(2) Discuss relationships at school: pupil/teacher, pupil/headmaster.
(3) Contrast these with relationships in offices: junior/senior, junior/boss.
(4) Discuss qualities apart from technical skill necessary to make an efficient secretary.
(5) Discuss this question from the point of view of an employer.

The tutor will arrive at the point when she can ask pupils to think of themselves applying for a job. How would they dress? Why would they be particular? What helps to create a favourable impression? How can they show themselves to best advantage?

She can then proceed to use role-play to help pupils recognise what may be deduced from displayed non-verbal behaviour.

First Exercise	An employer, three applicants.
Roles	Each applicant is applying for her first
Situation	job as a typist in a commercial firm.

Brief to class.—We are trying to discover what an employer may deduce about an applicant from the way in which she: knocks on a door, enters the office, walks across the floor, sits on a chair, answers a first greeting.

We will take the three applicants in turn and then we will discuss what we have observed and learned.

It may take one or two lessons to do this kind of preliminary work but if the tutor gears the work to the future then it is likely that interest will be maintained. On the other hand, all the points may be readily appreciated. Each tutor should proceed at the pace suitable for the class under instruction.

STAGE TWO

Go and see a local employer and find out from him the kind of questions he puts to applicants. Take a tape recorder and, if he is willing, interview him and get him to say what he is looking for when he interviews girls applying for posts in his firm. Most employers will be willing to co-operate in this way and a tape recording of the kind suggested will, when played back, bring an actual work situation into the school situation, and that is desirable.

STAGE THREE

In school

(1) Play back the employer's tape.

(2) Discuss with pupils the various points the employer made.

(3) Ask each pupil to think of herself in an office about to be asked a question at an interview. Of course, she will be addressed Miss So and So. For the time being therefore, she is not a pupil in a classroom but a young woman applying for a job.

(4) Assume role of employer and using a tape recorder ask each applicant in turn one of the questions put by the employer in the tape recording.

(5) Play back these recordings.

(6) Discuss the impression each applicant considered she created through the answering of her question. Consider matters such as: audibility, pleasantness of tone, degree of self confidence, clear answers to given questions.

(7) Repeat exercise to give opportunity for improvement.

(8) Evaluate nature and importance of pre-interview preparation.

STAGE FOUR: Follow-up

Set up a series of situations to give necessary practice.

The tutor may choose to play the role of employer in all the exercises but may consider it advisable to give students the opportunity to look at an interview through the eyes of an employer.

Encourage observation. Encourage the group to draw on their own experiences and to help each other to develop confidence.

Note: Interview procedure is considered in greater detail in Part Two.

COLLEGE SETTING: Students in college undergoing professional training.

A student group can be difficult to motivate, no matter the profession for which they are training. It is sensible, therefore, to recognise that there may be strong resistance to participation in role-play. Students accustomed to learning through lectures, seminars, discussions, may well view with considerable misgivings the prospect of having actually to *do* something in front of others. Uncooperative behaviour, however, may stem from anxiety, embarrassment or fear of losing face and not from any deliberate intention to be awkward.

The possible/probable reactions of students should be considered carefully by the tutor who intends to introduce role-play to such a group. It is difficult, however, to determine with any accuracy the feelings of others, and students in particular have highly developed defence-mechanisms which make assessment even more difficult. It should be recognised also that as a tutor moves further and further away in time from his or her own first experience of role-play it becomes increasingly difficult to remember what it felt like to be called upon to participate. Accordingly, tutors should not rely solely on their own observations or memories but should from time to time take steps to find the student point of view. Any such approach is likely to be possible only after students have come through initial difficulties, so the information a tutor gets from one group is for future reference.

The following conversation is a consequence of a tutor's desire to elicit reactions to role-play from students. The students in the conversation were taking a one-year post-graduate training in Youth and Community Work. In the third week of their first term they had been introduced to role-play by the tutor in the conversation. In the second term the four students elected to take a course on the uses of role-play and functions of the tutor. At the end of the third meeting of that course the tutor approached the students and asked if they would be prepared to take part in a conversation about role-play which would be recorded. They all agreed most willingly and the time was arranged for the period immediately following the next week's class. The speakers are referred to by initials: T is the tutor, B, F, L, S are students.

THE CONVERSATION

T. Thank you for agreeing to do this extra piece of work. May I ask this question first of all? Before coming into my class had you experienced role-play?

B. No.

L. Neither had I.

S. Nor I.

F. I had a bad experience when I was at my previous college: I was just terrified. I also had a good experience when working with kids last year. One of the Community Workers organised a role-play and it went very well. So I have seen it work well once.

T. At my third meeting with your group I asked you to role-play. What were your first reactions?

L. I came out in a cold sweat thinking that I'd have to get up in front of the whole group and do something and I didn't feel I could do that.

F. I felt like that as well. When we did our first role-play we hardly knew anyone in the group and that was the main worry for me.

T. Are you saying that the anxiety is less with the method and more with people?

B. Yes.

F. I would agree.

S. You get into a panic having to do something in front of others.

T. What makes that so difficult?

B. You are worried about how you are going to put yourself over and about what people are thinking of you.

S. I think it is perhaps the tension of wanting to portray something that will be acceptable, and yet not wanting to portray anything really about your central self. You feel exposed.

T. What would be a comfortable size of group for a first experience of role-play?

L. Four or five people.

T. I asked you to operate in buzz groups initially and then we moved into bigger groups of six or seven that contained observers. Were you asked to go into bigger groups too soon?

F. So far as I was concerned—yes. The absence of observers in the buzz groups helped and in the bigger group the conscious thought of people sitting watching was frightening. I lost confidence.

It is sensible to choose a method of introduction that causes least embarrassment and is closest to familiar methods of learning. The ideas advanced for the teachers could well be tried out for students. In particular, the *buzz group method* is to be recommended for although students may find it difficult to take the given simulated situation seriously, they are likely to appreciate the relative security of a buzz group. Two other suggestions are made: (*a*) the *Press Conference* and (*b*) the *Pair-role*.

PRESS CONFERENCE.   What to do:

(1)   Choose a newspaper article that has relevance for the group.
(2)   Read article to group, changing names, etc. to protect individuals and places mentioned in the article. (Let us suppose that the article reported conflict between a headmaster and parents on the question of school uniform.)
(3)   Choose sufficient students to cover persons mentioned in the article.
(4)   Allocate the different roles to them e.g. headmaster; two parents.
(5)   Ask role-takers to sit in front of the group as for a Press Conference.
(6)   Brief the group: 'Here we have the persons concerned in the dispute. The rest of us have opportunity to question them about their actions. We are concerned to understand, not to judge.'
(7)   Questioning of headmaster and parents begins.

Notes

It is more than likely that the tutor will require to ask the first question, which may be along the following lines, 'Headmaster, you are reported as having taken very high-handed action in this matter. How do you respond to that accusation?' In all probability students will become involved and plenty of questions will be posed. In discussion afterwards some may well express surprise at the degree of involvement experienced. It may be possible then for the tutor to set up simple role-plays in small groups to give students opportunity to explore the possibilities of role-play as a method of learning. For the Press Conference to be a useful method of working those who assume roles and indeed those who ask questions must have sufficient knowledge of the issues contained within the article to sustain the exercise at a worthwhile level. This merely underlines the importance of choosing material within the range of the group under tutelage.

THE PAIR-ROLE

It can happen that students resist the idea of role-play because the tutor has made the device seem to them to be very complicated and unnatural. A seemingly casual approach can, therefore, be most productive. The pair-role is a good example of this style of introduction.

Imagine that a group of students are taking a course on methods of instruction. One student has chosen Safety on the Hills and he is aiming his instruction towards youth club members with little experience.

He has laid out his equipment and begins his instruction, during the course of which he tells the group what they should and should not do. At a particular moment the tutor, in the role of club member, asks for clarification, 'I didn't understand that bit—could you go over it again, please?' The student does so and the flow of his work continues.

Notes

Given such a lead another member of the group may ask a further question, but if not the tutor should let the matter rest there for the time being. However, prior to the next exercise the tutor would say, 'Try to help the instructor realise something of what it is like in real-life by asking the kind of questions you think members of his chosen learning group would pose.'

Questions will come. Some may be a bit silly at first and the instructor may or may not be able to cope. Either way there is material for discussion.

Once the method of working is established and felt to be helpful it can be labelled role-play and the technique described more fully if it is important to do so.

There are many people who have used role-play in teaching programmes without realising this was what they were doing. The method was given a name by sociologists but it was not invented by them.

iii SOCIAL SETTINGS

Advice has been given on the introduction of role-play to persons for whom the tutor had some educational responsibility, and in all the examples quoted he or she has operated from a recognised position within each particular group.

Under this heading more informal methods of introduction will be considered, with the tutor not necessarily having educational responsibility for those with whom he or she will work.

Certain important differences should be noted:

(1) Occurring in a social environment as against an educational one, the decision to use role-play is often prompted by circumstances.

(2) The three stages—Briefing, Interaction, Discussion are not always apparent.

(3) Use of observers is limited.

(4) The tutor operates by invitation more often than not.

Examples now to be considered should make these points clear.

FIRST EXAMPLE: A Personal Problem

In conversation with Mary at the Youth Club one evening, the leader noticed that she appeared to be worried about something. She had an opportunity to talk to Mary alone. It transpired that Mary's mother wanted her to stay on at school but Mary's wish was to leave at the end of the summer term when she would be sixteen. Mary wanted to be a hairdresser and was in fact already in a salon every Saturday and two week nights after school. She enjoyed the work very much but knew that her mother thought of the work as temporary: she wanted her daughter to stay at school and get some useful qualification. Most of Mary's friends were leaving with job prospects. The salon was prepared to take Mary on full time if she left school at sixteen. Mary was very fond of her mother and did not want to upset her but she was ready to leave school and start doing what she ,wanted to do. The leader and Mary talked over the problem for a little while and then the leader said, 'Convince me. I'll put your mother's point of view and see if you can persuade me that you really know your own mind'. During the role-play the leader, in the role of mother, tested and questioned. She put forward likely objections and arguments. Mary coped fairly well at first but when she was about to lose her temper with her 'mother' the leader broke off the interaction.

In the conversation after the role-play Mary recognised that to have a head-on clash with her mother would get her nowhere and she came to acknowledge the validity of some of the arguments that her mother might advance. Maybe as a consequence Mary went into the conversation with her mother in a more mature manner and perhaps with greater awareness of her mother's point of view.

Although, in print, this method of working within a conversational framework may appear to be rather contrived and unnatural, in practice, if appropriately timed, it is not so. On such occasions the choice lies with the one seeking advice either to accept or reject the role-play. In our example, Mary responded to the suggestion 'Convince me as I speak for your mother' because no doubt, at that particular moment she felt it would be helpful. Had she felt differently the offer would have been rejected and 'normal' conversation would have continued.

There are occasions when one person assuming the appropriate pair-role can help another person prepare for some future encounter. For instance:

A   seeks permission from his employer for leave of absence to participate in an international tournament.

B   is due to see a particular person to try to persuade her to refrain from taking a certain course of action.

C   is seeking help from a head teacher for a particular project.

D   is due to go for an interview.

Such a role-play could well be helpful in the presentation of a 'case' and in dealing with observations or questions that could be advanced in the real encounter.

SECOND EXAMPLE: A Common Problem

At a community centre a group of young people were sitting drinking coffee and talking about their holidays. The warden of the centre joined the group and was brought into the conversation. Where was he going for his holiday and where were they? One member talked about going abroad and that started off discussion on going into restaurants—menus in French, confusing cutlery, ordering a meal, ordering wines. Emerging from this the warden asked someone to fetch some cutlery, and there and then he set up a table and gave instruction on the placing and use of cutlery. The lesson developed into a role-play with the warden taking the role of waiter and others playing the role of customers, during which advice was given on the ordering of meals, on seeking the opinion of a waiter on the choice of wine, on paying the bill, and on tipping.

Following the role-play there was an interesting discussion on eating out—dutch treats, etc.

If the young people had not wished to discuss matters with the warden the opportunity to use role-play would not have arisen. Equally had the group not been entertained by the thought of pretending to be in a restaurant the warden's 'Will you fetch some cutlery and I'll show you what I mean' would have had a different response.

In this case, however, stemming from the discussion, the warden, on the basis of what he thought would be a favourable response, made a suggestion which was accepted. The experience was most enjoyable: everyone laughed a lot and got some useful information.

The introduction of role-play to persons unfamiliar with the device should be based upon a tutor's assessment of circumstances, including:

(1) Nature, needs and number of persons with whom the tutor will be working.
(2) Environment in which the work will occur.
(3) Nature of the authority that the tutor has in relation to the persons with whom he or she will be working.
(4) Tutor's reasons for using the device.

No claim is made that methods given in illustration and used as models will work. Examples are intended to give information on matters that influence choice and to provide ideas that might be developed to meet individual requirements.

PART TWO

There are five sections in Part Two. Each section deals with the application of role-play against the background of declared training circumstances.

The first four sections should be of particular interest to teachers and the final one to those engaged in Youth and Community work. However, many of the exercises, suitably adapted, would be as appropriate for one training group as for another.

Sections

1. Preparation of students for the teaching profession (p.68)
2. Development of conversational skills (p.91)
3. Subject teaching (p.127)
4. School to work (p.134)
5. Youth and Community training courses. (p.141)

PART TWO : SECTION ONE

PREPARATION OF STUDENTS FOR THE TEACHING PROFESSION

Teaching is a complex activity. It could be described as a process which engages teachers and learners in a cooperative effort to reach educational goals. Teachers are expected to be able to deal competently with all aspects of the process and in practice this means that they are called upon to:

(a) exercise control of self and of own behaviour towards pupils
(b) be aware of interaction within the classroom and being aware to respond appropriately
(c) be in command of subject knowledge
(d) be sufficiently flexible in approach and method to meet needs of the particular pupils of the moment
(e) try to understand feelings, attitudes and difficulties of pupils
(f) encourage pupils to try to reach goals commensurate with potential.

This is a formidable task embracing, as it does, not only skill in teaching methods but also skills necessary for the maintenance of effective relationships.

It is in the area of human relations that role-play could make a particularly valuable contribution in training as by the very nature of the device there is opportunity for students to engage in dynamic encounters. Through involvement in exercises students have opportunity to arrive at a fuller understanding of interaction and perhaps come closer to the total teaching process than is possible from their own reading and studying and even, maybe, from observing others teach.

Exercises in this section are offered, therefore, with the aim of giving tutors ideas for use of role-play in the preparation of students for the classroom.

Different areas of the teaching process are considered and exercises for the development of skills are offered. The areas are: i observation, ii interpersonal communication, iii factors that influence, iv classroom interaction, and v practising the role.

Exercises in each area are grouped in sets and each set has a common training objective.

i OBSERVATION

The verb 'to observe' is taken to mean, 'to take notice of' or 'to be conscious of'. Observation calls into action all the senses but for teachers particularly those of sight and hearing. Having defined the term let us identify the problem. The problem is double-edged. Send students out on a visit to schools with instructions to observe teachers in action with pupils, and the chances are that much of the interaction will go unnoticed for, in the normal course of living, people do not necessarily take any special note of the different signals that coexist in face-to-face interaction or of the effect that the behaviour of one person has upon others.

These same students, however, believing in their own infallibility, may well come to snap judgements about pupils, teachers and relationships based on what they have noticed. Any training, therefore, has to be concerned not only with perception but also with interpretation.

As a first task, a tutor may well have to persuade students that taking notice of behaviour is crucial to their competence as teachers, for many are likely to give development of observational skills little attention unless encouraged to do so. With this in mind, the first set contains 'warm-up' exercises designed primarily to arouse interest.

FIRST SET: Warm-up

EXERCISE A

Objectives   To stimulate interest.
              To promote discussion on perception.

Exercise   Certain students are briefed to act in specific ways. The remainder of the group are asked one by one to observe for a given period of time and then to answer questions put to them.

1.   Sub-divide group into observers and demonstrators.
2.   Observers leave room to return singly.
3.   Give specific instructions to demonstrators emphasising need for accuracy.
4.   Demonstrators take up given positions. (See diagram.)
5.   First observer is called back into room and asked to stand with back to demonstrators.
6.   Explain to observer that 30 seconds will be given for looking at the people at the other end of the room.
7.   Ask observer to turn round. Demonstrators behave as per instructions.
8.   After 30 seconds ask observer to turn back and face you. Demonstrators stop action.
9.   Put prepared questions to observer.

10. Record each answer.
11. Ask observer to take a seat in the room well away from demonstrators.
12. Deal similarly with all observers.
13. Go over recorded answers with total group and check with reality.
14. General discussion.

Positions given to demonstrators.

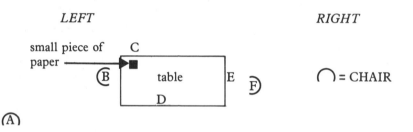

Positions

A   sits on chair left of table and apart from the others.
B   sits on chair at the left end of table.
C   stands above table.
D   sits on front edge of table.
E   leans against right end of table.
F   sits on chair right which is turned in towards table.

Other Instructions

A   sits still, looking forward throughout demonstrations. A's watch is the
     only one visible.
B   and D talk together.
C   keeps right hand on piece of paper; listens to B/D conversation; shows
     interest but does not speak
E   talks to F. Is asked to take off glasses (which are worn normally) and to
     hide them before demonstration begins.
F   listens to E. After 5 seconds takes out pen and clicks it for remainder of
     30 seconds.

Questions

Who was speaking to whom?
How many were sitting in chairs?
What was A wearing?
Was anyone touching anything apart from themselves or furniture?
How many were wearing spectacles?
What movements occurred?
How many watches were visible?
How many different colours of shoes were there?

Teaching Points

Experience has shown this to be a most enjoyable exercise and one that gives rise to a range of most valuable comments particularly in the area of selective perception. In addition it sets people off in a frame of mind conducive to future work in the development of observational skills.

A useful next step is to help students appreciate the difference between factual and impressionistic observations. The following exercise has that in mind.

EXERCISE B

Objectives To draw distinction between facts and impressions.
What to do Acquire a picture or a photograph of a group of people engaged one with another in some activity.

Show this picture to the group and ask each member to list three or four aspects of the picture that are factual, e.g. four people are standing near each other; two children are apart from the adults.

When lists have been made, ask members to draw a line underneath the factual list, to make any deductions on the basis of their listed facts; and to record these, e.g. that the conversation is so interesting that none of the adults is concerned about the children.

In turn each student should give one listed fact. Some facts may have been inaccurately observed. For instance one student may have listed three adults, failing to observe that a fourth is slightly hidden. Discuss implications.

Proceed to ask students to give their interpretation of the facts and then move into discussion on differences between facts and impressions. This is an important lesson for students to learn as it is all too easy for teachers (and others) to fall into the trap of thinking that the interpretation they put on a pupil's behaviour is the true one. From other sources students will possibly have gained knowledge of such matters as selective perception and human fallibility. The warm-up exercises should, therefore, both reinforce and extend knowledge.

SECOND SET: Observation of Interaction

Main Objective

To give students practice in the recognition of inter-personal signals in dynamic circumstances.

EXERCISE A

Certain students engage in conversation while the remainder look and listen.
  Steps to take:
  (1) Before class commences, draw up a list of questions for guidance of observers.
  (2) Sub-divide group As to engage in conversation, Bs to observe.
  (3) Ask As to choose own topic for their conversation.
  (4) Give to each observer a copy of the questionnaire and ask them to record answers.
  (5) Allow time for observers to look at own questionnaire.
       Sample questionnaire:
           Who spoke first?
           How many members of the group never spoke at all?
           Which members of the group spoke most frequently?
           What did you notice about the non-verbal behaviour of _____?
           (fill in one name)
           What effect do you consider that _____'s (same name) behaviour had upon other members of the group?
  (6) Interaction/observation.
  (7) When appropriate stop interaction.
  (8) Give observers time to finish their own recording.
  (9) Ask for observations.
  (10) General discussion.

Teaching points

The idea of giving questions to observers is useful as it does help beginners to focus on particular aspects of interaction and to some extent avoids unproductive, haphazard looking and/or over-concentration upon content.

In addition by isolating one person for each observer's special attention more detailed observation of non-verbal signals is encouraged.

By the very nature of the questions there will be further opportunity for the tutor to draw distinction between facts and impressions. For instance, the person who spoke first and the number of any who did not speak at all are facts whether noticed or not. Why someone spoke first or never spoke at all are impressions—opinions based on what had been noticed but not necessarily accurate assessments of feelings/attitudes.

Sub-groups may be changed round and first exercise repeated with a different questionnaire, based perhaps on how observers coped in the first run of the exercise.

EXERCISE B

What to do; Preparation; determine task and make up one role-card per person.

(1) Divide group into two units. As role-play. Bs observe.
(2) Read out the task. For example, the As are members of the School Magazine Committee. A special meeting has been called to consider a suggestion that due to failure of pupils to submit articles the Magazine be discontinued for this session.
(3) Ask the observers (the Bs) to retire out of ear-shot and to make any preparation necessary for their own observation of interaction.
(4) Place role-cards face down and ask As to select one each.

A1. You are the chairman. A3 made the suggestion. You will call upon A3 to speak on his proposal before opening the meeting for general discussion. You do not support the suggestion, but you are in the chair.

A2. You have not made up your mind but you think that, once dropped, the Magazine would be difficult to resurrect. You do not get on well with A3.

A3. You made the suggestion. You have been in touch with the pupils and you claim that the majority show no interest in the Magazine. You do not like A2.

A4. You think that probably it would be a good idea to give the Magazine a rest for a year but you do dislike arguments.

A5. You are for the suggestion and are very keen that the Magazine should be dropped. It would mean much less work for you.

A6. You are quite opposed and question A3's statement that pupils are not interested.

(5) Members of committee complete their own briefing and share information given on role cards concerning relationships. This should take a matter of minutes only.

(6) While As prepare, brief Bs, for instance:
Each member of the committee has been given a role, information which is hidden from you. You are required to observe interaction. Try to remain detached from the arguments and the persons who are advancing them so that you may be able to concentrate on the inter-play. Get yourselves into a position where you can see what is going on. When it is over you will be asked for observations. Do not rely on memory. Take notes.

(7) When everyone is ready and the room set out to accommodate members of a committee in session—the chairman (i.e. A1) begins.

(8) At a suitable moment stop interaction: call for comments from observers and make the necessary learning points.

Teaching points

The exercise is not designed to teach chairmanship nor committee procedure so it is important not to be diverted into these areas. The role-playing may have been somewhat extreme and if that has happened and it has moved beyond the bounds of plausibility the interaction will have been easily recognised. The more subtle the inter-play the more difficult is the task of the observers, so in either case there will be discussion material.

If appropriate, organise a similar exercise to give Group A opportunity to observe. Quite often this will not be necessary as there will be opportunity to develop observational skills in all subsequent exercises which a tutor introduces.

ii INTER-PERSONAL COMMUNICATION

Exercises in this area are very simple. Although students may find them quite entertaining they do give rise to discussion that has considerable relevance for their future work as teachers.

Main objectives

To give students the opportunity to appreciate:

  (i)   the visual and vocal signals that coexist with verbal ones in conversations.
  (ii) the extent to which they rely on the non-verbal to convey intention and to interpret the intention of others.
  (iii) the importance of such signals in the maintenance of inter-personal communication.
  (iv) the capacity of pupils to interpret non-verbal signals emanating from the teacher.
  (v)   the problems of the listener and factors that affect concentration.

Three exercises are offered: in each, students work in buzz groups calling themselves A, B, or C.

FIRST EXERCISE

As and Bs remain in room. Cs leave the room.

Brief As and Bs.

   When Cs join their own buzz group each group will engage in a conversation on, let's say, music. The object of the exercise is for each of you to feel what it is like to talk only through words. So far as possible, therefore, eliminate all visual signals and try to cut down vocal variety. This will mean avoiding eye contact with C, giving no nods and smiles and cutting out hand gestures. It will also mean using a bland tone of voice that conveys little enthusiasm or interest. All very difficult to do—but try. I shall tell the Cs that you have been asked to talk with them about music but I shall not tell them of the restrictions placed upon your behaviour. Remember to be chatty in verbal terms. Get a seat ready for your own C.

Go outside to brief Cs

   When you enter you will see where your own group is and you should join it. Your As and Bs have been asked to talk with you on the subject of music. You are asked to engage with them in conversation.

Interaction. Cs join their own group and conversations begin.

From response, judge amount of time to be given to interaction. As a guide, 5 minutes might suffice.

Discussion. Stop interaction and ask each group to talk within their own group and in particular to consider the effect that virtual elimination of non-verbal signals had upon behaviour. Give time for such discussions.

Invite comments from students. Comments may well include:

1. It was very difficult to talk without using my hands.
2. I dried up because neither A nor B seemed at all interested.
3. We all felt quite embarrassed.
4. It was hilarious—we just laughed.
5. I didn't realise just how much I do rely on gestures and facial expressions when in conversation.
6. I found that because I was trying to cut out gestures etc., I couldn't think of words to say. My mind seemed to go blank.
7. If people don't look interested and don't smile at you it's very off-putting.
8. I had to sit on my hands.
9. Gestures can get you out of trouble when you don't know what to say or can't say it.
10. I found conversation impossible and I really got quite angry with the other two.

SECOND EXERCISE

As go outside. Bs and Cs remain in room.

Brief Bs and Cs. You are asked to accept that a group of strangers are in town and each pair of you has agreed to entertain one stranger for the evening. The only information that you have is that the strangers are all students. What are you going to suggest to your guest? You plan the evening while I brief the As.

Go outside to brief As. Tell them what you have told Bs and Cs. Emphasise that so far as they—the As—are concerned there is no deception. However what the 'insiders' do not know is that the strangers are all foreign students and neither speak nor understand English. Tell As that as they are all intelligent people they should respond to visual cues. Further, that if an A speaks another language and this is discovered, conversation in that language may proceed. Briefing is completed, As join their own group.

Interaction. After a further 5 or so minutes stop interaction and again give time for separate discussions before inviting comments.

Possible comments

1. We found ourselves shouting to try to make ourselves understood.
2. I felt excluded because B and C turned to each other so often and talked *ABOUT* me.
3. We reduced everything to basics. Not 'Would you like to go for a drink' but 'Drink?' plus gesture.
4. Everything was so exaggerated.
5. I managed very well because A and I discovered we could talk in German.
   Yes, and that made me feel the outsider.
6. When people don't understand what you are saying you tend to think that they are stupid.
7. We worked on the assumption that our A was deaf and then we treated her as if she had little intelligence.

Encourage students to consider implication of their observations in the context of teaching.

From the two exercises draw attention to:

1. Type of information that is conveyed through tone of voice, expressions, gestures, etc.
2. Extent to which the non-verbal helps in the understanding of intention.
3. What a teacher may reveal to pupils non-verbally.
4. Problem, therefore, of trying to conceal irritation or worse from pupils who may be slow to respond or slow to learn.
5. Pupil reaction to raised voices.
6. The 'does he take sugar?' syndrome.
7. Importance of the non-verbal in the encouragement of communication.

THIRD EXERCISE

Still in buzz groups.

This exercise is concerned with listening and non-verbal response behaviour. Ask Bs in each group to talk to their own A and C, without interruption for about 10 minutes. While Bs are making up their minds on topic, brief As and Cs.

Brief. You should make a real effort to concentrate from start to finish on what your B is saying.

As, you are asked to listen as you would normally using response nods, smiles etc., as appropriate.

Cs, you are asked also to listen throughout but not to convey the impression of listening. For instance, you could slouch in your chair, gaze at the ceiling, shift around, keep head down, you decide on your own behaviour.

Interaction. Bs give their talks. At the end of the given time stop proceedings.

Discussion. Within each group ask each B (the speaker) to give own impression of the the two listeners and to say how their behaviour affected his/her performance when speaking. Ask each listener to talk about his/her own listening pattern; to declare distractions and to indicate the extent to which they were able/willing to ignore them.

GENERAL DISCUSSION

Ask students to reflect on such matters as are contained in the following questions.

How necessary to the speaker are the non-verbal responses of listeners?
Are teachers affected by the lack of response from pupils?
Can a teacher always tell when a pupil is listening?
Will pupils always say if they have not understood what has been said?
What would be some reasons for concealment?
How does interest in the speaker's topic affect listening?
Does concentration come and go even when the topic is commanding attention?
Do factors like weather, time of day, day of week, temperature of room, affect the behaviour of teachers?
Are pupils affected by similar distractions?
Should pupils be able to ignore distractions?

Teaching points

It is relatively easy to acquire theoretical information about behaviour—there are a variety of books on the subject. Students, no doubt, will receive lectures on aspects of inter-personal behaviour in the classroom.

It is also fairly easy to recognise what others do but quite difficult to be aware of one's own behaviour.

The value of these exercises lies in the fact that they provide experiences from which students are able to recognise not only what they do themselves but also how their behaviour has affected others. Subsequent discussion gives students an opportunity to reflect upon their own behaviour in relation to pupils.

iii FACTORS THAT INFLUENCE

FIRST SET: Personal Space

Why do theatregoers feel better pleased when they are surrounded by people and not by empty seats?

Why will people in a crowded bus or tube stand close together seemingly undisturbed by the contact?

Why is annoyance often displayed when a stranger sits at a table that is already occupied if there are vacant tables in the restaurant?

Why do people when about to sit in a chair in a strange environment often adjust the position of the chair?

Such questions are concerned with personal space, as are the exercises in this set.

EXERCISE A

Ask five students to stand at one end of the room (Row A).

Ask five other students to take up positions at the other end of the room and directly opposite someone in row A.

Assuming that there are twelve students in the total group the remaining two would be asked to observe.

Students in Row A should be asked to stand still and remain still throughout.

Students in Row B should be asked to walk slowly towards the opposite person in row A until each is directly in front of his or her partner.

Meantime, observers watch.

That being done, Bs return to their original position and then As walk slowly towards Bs similarly.

Ask for comments and these may include:

(1)   There was a fair amount of avoidance behaviour.
(2)   Few pairs were able to maintain eye contact throughout although in the second run this was better.
(3)   There was quite a bit of what appeared to be embarassed giggling.
(4)   No one spoke.
(5)   No one shook hands with the approaching partner.
(6)   Some pairs seemed more uncomfortable the closer they got to each other.

Teaching points

If this exercise is used, participating students will be faced with the unknown—and will react in certain ways. Maybe some will feel very foolish. Maybe a few will be able to maintain their composure. Let students reflect upon their own behaviour and then go on to consider the responsibility of the teacher in relation to pupils who may be experiencing feelings of insecurity as they are asked to face the unknown, unfamiliar or difficult.

Emphasise the need to be alert to the different non-verbal cues that give outward signs of inner anxiety.

The next exercise is set in the classroom and is intended to focus attention upon personal space in the classroom.

EXERCISE B: Personal space in the classroom.
Roles Teacher, pupils.

For this exercise the tutor should play the role of teacher.
(1) Arrange seating as a classroom.
(2) Choose content of lesson.
(3) Determine age of pupils (top primary or secondary).
(4) Begin to teach.
(5) Ask pupils to take notes (or any written task consistent with lesson) During the course of teaching the teacher should occupy different positions in the classroom and go through certain actions, for example:
   (*a*) Begin by sitting behind desk.
   (*b*) Rise and move close to the nearest pupils.
   (*c*) Turn away and write on blackboard (still teaching).
   (*d*) Turn round and sit on desk.
   (*e*) Rise and move to back of room behind pupils.
   (*f*) Remain there for some time.
   (*g*) Move forward and stand over one pupil to see what he or she is doing.
   (*h*) Move into position to see what another pupil is doing. Bend over pupil.
   (*i*) Return to front.
   (*j*) Finish teaching.
(6) Ask students for their reactions.
(7) Pose certain questions, possibly:
   (*a*) Does the position a teacher takes up in the classroom have any significance?
   (*b*) Is there a comfortable/productive distance between teacher and pupils?
   (*c*) Does this vary? With age? With sex?

(*d*) Has the movement of the teacher any effect upon pupils?
(*e*) To what extent can distance be bridged through eye contact?
(*f*) If pupils have to sit close together in a crowded classroom what, if any, effect might this have upon them?
(*g*) Is a desk a symbol of authority?
(*h*) Does a desk offer protection to pupils?

SECOND SET: Voices

Ask students to talk about vocal behaviour and the tendency will be for them to concentrate upon word selection, pronunciation, clarity, fluency and perhaps projection, for it is generally held that matters such as these are the most important aspects of voices in the classroom.

Listen to pupils talking about teachers' voices and you may hear:

'So and so has a very nice voice.'
'Her voice gets on my nerves.'
'He drones on and on—it's so boring.'
'I wish she wouldn't shout at me.'
'I could listen to him for hours.'
'I hate his voice.'

Teachers are apt to consider voices more in relation to thinking than feeling, quite forgetting that a voice makes an emotional impact upon a listener which in turn affects that person's capacity/desire to think and act.

Students must appreciate that their voices will affect the behaviour of pupils and in turn they will be affected by the voices of their pupils.

Role-play exercises offered are designed to help students:

(*a*) recognise personal preferences
(*b*) appreciate need to control bias
(*c*) understand the part human sounds play in influencing communication.

EXERCISE A

(1) Prepare a tape in which 4 or 5 people with markedly different speaking
.   styles each in turn read the same passage.
(2) Without any indication of reason for so doing, play the tape.
(3) Ask students for their reactions.
(4) Discuss (*a*) personal preferences
              (*b*) responses to human sounds
              (*c*) impressions gained on the evidence of voice alone.
   Is beauty all in the ear of the listener?

(5) Consider (*a*) implications in relation to the voices of pupils
                 (*b*) reactions of pupils to the voices of teachers.

EXERCISE B

The main idea behind this exercise is to give students opportunity to reflect
upon the reciprocal nature of vocal interaction.
(1) Ask students to work in pairs and to engage in short exercises of the
    following nature:

  (*a*)   Brief As to ask Bs six questions using a strong, forceful voice
          throughout questioning.
  (*b*)   Brief Bs to talk to As as if speaking to a child.
  (*c*)   Brief As to adopt a timid voice and to engage Bs in conversation.
  (*d*)   Brief Bs—you did not want to do this job but you have been
          instructed to ask the As six questions and the whole business
          bores you.
  (*e*)   Brief As to explain something to Bs. Then independently brief Bs
          to pretend not to understand what their own A is saying.
  (*f*)   Brief Bs to tell some story to As. Then brief As to argue.

The various exercises proceed simultaneously and although students will
know that each exercise is a 'put-up job' they are likely to be willing to
participate and to learn from their experiences.

Encourage each pair to discuss reactions.

Remind students that pupils are quick to interpret and respond to what is
being said to them non-verbally.

Maybe in the exercises a low level of tolerance was displayed and in that
event remind students that as teachers they will be at the receiving end of non-
verbal comments and may, therefore, require to develop greater emotional
control.

No speaker can *FORCE* another person to engage in interaction although
he may be successful through his behaviour in persuading the other person to
engage.

No speaker can *MAKE* a pupil listen. That is a decision which a pupil
makes for himself. All that a teacher can hope to do is through his own
appreciation of the listener's problems address himself to the task of trying to
minimise difficulties and maximise motivation.

The following exercises should identify some difficulties that listeners may
experience in relation to voices.

EXERCISE C

(1) Prepare a tape in which two people engage in conversation.
(2) Play back tape.
(3) Increase volume beyond what was considered necessary at the outset.
(4) Bring back volume to normal.
(5) Reduce volume, making listening difficult.
(6) Pick up volume again.

Discuss reactions.

Focus on: Hearing loss that individual pupils may experience.
　　　　　 Effect shouting may have on pupils.
　　　　　 Possible consequence in general tension if voices are consistently
　　　　　 loud: quiet: strident: apologetic, etc.,

EXERCISE D

(1) Prepare a tape in which two persons with pronounced foreign accents
converse in English.
(2) Play back tape and after approximately 10 SECONDS arrest tape and pose
questions:
What have you understood of content?
What prevented you from fuller understanding?
(It is likely that some students will have found the unfamiliar voices too
great a barrier and will not have been able to comment on content. Of
those who were able to focus on content some will have understood more
than others. A few may have found the tape so annoying they stopped
listening.)
(3) Start the tape again and ask each student to indicate the point in the conversation when he or she was able to concentrate upon content.

Discuss:
(a) importance of 'tuning in' to voices and of giving advance knowledge of
what is to come
(b) connection between interest and attention
(c) connection between physical comfort and attention.

(*Notes*: The main reason for using tape recordings is that the focus is on
sound. The problem of a teacher's speaking style being in sharp contrast to
those of pupils is discussed fully in the following section.)

Teaching points

When listening to a speaker people have a saturation point beyond which
nothing much registers very clearly.

Concentration span varies with individuals and with their knowledge and interest in, the topic, and perhaps also the speaker and/or the occasion.

Speakers tend to over-estimate the listening capacity of an audience. Teachers, perhaps especially, are apt to talk too much in their efforts to get as much across as possible in the time available. This can be counter-productive.

Silence is not just the absence of sound. It is an aspect of communication that might be used more effectively in the classroom. For example, if the silence which follows the impact of a fresh idea or the reading of a poem is broken too soon it prejudices any excitement or enjoyment which individual pupils may be experiencing. Teachers encourage pupils to think and to use their imaginations, and thus the timing of any intervention into the silent world of thought requires care.

The exercises that have been offered under the heading Factors that Influence, and perhaps particularly those that have been concerned with *voices*, are important because they bring students into areas that are fundamental to effective classroom interaction.

The more students know about the effect that their speaking has upon others the better equipped they are to encourage cooperation from pupils. In addition, the more they are aware of their own personal prejudices in relation to the voices and speaking of others the more likely they are to exercise the necessary control of bias.

This, of course, ties up with observation. The first requisite is the capacity to observe reactions, and the second is to have the will and the ability to adjust behaviour accordingly.

The following story which a teacher told against herself may serve as a reminder that the interpretative skills of pupils are considerable.

> When I first started to teach in a Special School where the pupils were mentally handicapped I disliked the work, but I believed I was keeping my thoughts to myself. How wrong I was! At the end of my first term I said to the class, 'I hope you all have a very happy Christmas and I look forward to seeing you next term.' A pupil replied, 'You won't Miss. You don't like us.'

iv CLASSROOM INTERACTION

Having broken down interaction into certain components and helped students to appreciate their significance, it is time now to let students put it all together again in the total teaching process.

Exercises in this area involve students in simulated situations. They are intended to give them the feel of relating to pair-roles. The exercises are short, simple and well within capability. It is important that, at this stage in preparation for the classroom, confidence should be built up. For this reason the tutor should ask the pair-roles to present no disciplinary problems, unless specifically asked to do so.

Initially students may find it difficult to play the pair-role in the teacher-pupil relationship. So it may be helpful if the tutor suggests to students playing the pupil role that they only respond in verbal terms. In other words they are not required to portray all the aspects of pupil-behaviour that might take place in similar situations in the classroom. Emphasis is not upon the playing of pair-roles except in so far as this provides learning experience for student teachers.

FIRST SET
EXERCISE A

Task

> To give to the class directions that require pupils to take specific action. For example, a change in the timetable means that pupils must bring certain items of equipment to school the following day.

Sample questions to pose after interaction:

> Did pupils understand directions, did they know what was being asked of them?
> Were steps taken to try to ensure that pupils did understand?
> Was opportunity given for pupils to check that they had the correct information?
> Were pupils' questions dealt with satisfactorily?

EXERCISE B

Same teacher and same pupils. The next day. Directions were not obeyed by all pupils. Deal with the situation.
Questions:

> How did the teacher handle the situation?
> Were defaulters given opportunity to explain?
> Did pupils feel they had been fairly treated?

EXERCISE C

Elicit information from 'pupils' on a subject of the 'Teacher's' own choice.
Questions:

> Were pupils encouraged to talk?
> Did pupils consider the teacher was interested in what they were saying?
> What did the teacher do that gave the impression she really was listening?
> Did any pupil feel left out?

4

EXERCISE D

Tell a story.
Questions:
    Did you feel you had the pupils with you all the time?
    What did you do initially to try to concentrate their attention?
    Some pupils seemed to be restless. Why?
    You showed a picture at one point. Did everyone see it?
    If everyone cannot see properly, what are some possible reactions?
    What are the dangers of over-stimulation?

SECOND SET

Repeat exercises but introduce degrees of difficulty stemming from the behaviour of pupils. It is advisable that tutors should place some restriction on behaviour to ensure that actions do not prejudice learning. Challenges must be met but challenge unrelated to ability can sap confidence.
    Behaviour that might be introduced with benefit:
(*a*) Attempts to divert the teacher from main task.
(*b*) Posing of awkward questions.
(*c*) Chatting to neighbours when silence is expected.
(*d*) Appearing uninterested.
After each exercise the 'teacher' should be given opportunity to comment on own performance.

Teaching points

The baiting of teachers is almost a recognised sport and it might be interesting to elicit from the students if they felt they had the teacher 'on the ropes' during the interaction and whether or not they derived any pleasure from so doing.

Having someone at your mercy requires considerable self-control if advantage is not to be taken of that position. Students should be encouraged to be as honest as possible about their own feelings as 'pupils' for in so doing they may come to a fuller understanding of the problems they may face when as teachers they encounter awkward/difficult/troublesome pupils.

Whether or not the tutor takes part in the exercises as a pupil would be a matter of choice and yet it has to be said that there are distinct advantages to be gained from the role-reversal. Certainly if the tutor is not prepared to be at risk the chances of students being willing to be so are remote. The tutor should be prepared to lay his own skills in human relationships 'on the line' and this could be the factor that encourages committed work from students.

Although the work has serious intent it does not need to be seriously conducted. If students and tutor enjoy working together, the chances are that more will be accomplished. Laughter and good humour are important ingredients.

v PRACTISING THE ROLE

OBJECTIVES

To give students opportunities to teach in simulated situations and thus to provide students with opportunity to:

(a) prepare a lesson for a particular class of pupils
(b) perceive and learn from their own actions
(c) learn from the experience of being a pupil
(d) develop capacity to cope with the unexpected.

FIRST SET OF EXERCISES

Main objectives

To give students opportunity to prepare a lesson and then teach it.

Select four students. Ask each to prepare a lesson which can be presumed to continue beyond the ten minutes allocated for each role-play.

Brief those who will play the role of pupils to be responsive.

Allocate two observers for each role-play.

Note: Give students a reasonable amount of time for preparation. For example, the tasks could be given out at one meeting of the group for under-taking at the next meeting.

Role-plays could follow without discussion but it might be advisable to give opportunity for discussion after each lesson. If the available time is one hour, five minute discussion could follow each role-play.

Each teacher should know whether the pupils consider that her material has been well prepared, interestingly presented and appropriate in terms of the supposed age and ability of the class.

SECOND SET OF EXERCISES

Main objectives

To give students an opportunity to prepare a lesson and to teach it to pupils who are showing some unwillingness to be involved.

Emphasis in this set is therefore upon the total process.

Select four other students to perform their tasks at the next meeting. Outline the task which is a progression of tasks in the first set, in that teachers will be asked to cope with less co-operative behaviour. Brief observers and pupils. Brief pupils to present problems for each teacher. If necessary, remind pupils that extreme behaviour is not required.

Brief observers to pay particular attention to matters such as the teacher's (a) self-control; (b) capacity to be aware of interaction and being aware to respond appropriately; (c) relationship with pupils.

DISCUSSION

Those who played the role of teacher should be encouraged to talk about any difficulties they experience in the role. There should be a sharing of information stemming from the desire of students to assist each other to develop confidence and skills.

Relevant questions for each teacher to consider after role-play might be:

(a) Could you recognise signals emanating from pupils?

(b) Were you aware of the effect your behaviour had on pupils?

(c) To what extent were you able to monitor your own behaviour?

(d) Did you ever feel you were losing the class?

(e) If so, do you know what contributed to their movement away?

(f) What would you wish to remember from your experience?

Relevant questions for pupils to consider after interaction:

(a) Did the teacher do or say anything that made learning more difficult for you?

(b) Did you consider the teacher was trying to encourage you to learn?

(c) If so, what gave you that impression?

(d) When your behaviour was unco-operative how did you feel the teacher related to you?

THIRD SET OF EXERCISES AFTER FIRST TEACHING PRACTICE

Objective

To give students further opportunities to practise the role in the light of any difficulties experienced when on teaching practice.

1. Give students an opportunity to discuss difficulties and to compare experiences.

2. Ask students to complete this sentence:

When on teaching practice I found it difficult to . . .

3. Arrange for three students each to undertake the following task at next meeting.

Task

Prepare a lesson that can be presumed to continue beyond the allotted time of ten minutes. Choose a set of circumstances based on declared difficulty.

4. Give opportunity for all students to undertake a similar task.

Teaching points

The student playing the role of teacher sets up her own exercise. A student may have chosen to be a pupil in her own exercise. In every exercise information given in the briefing will have a basis in fact and role-takers will be expected to respond according to their brief. Obviously there will be only an approximation of the real-life interaction. Exercises, therefore, should be seen as points of departure for discussion.

The sharing of information and particularly that gained from teaching practice should be encouraged.

FINAL SET OF EXERCISES

Exercises in this final set are considered to be suitable for students at an advanced stage of training. Not all of the teacher's work is concerned with groups of pupils and so the exercises in this set are designed to give students information in one to one relationships. In each exercise two students participate, one as teacher and the other as pupil while the remainder observe. It may well be, however, that in an exercise the tutor is allocated a role.

Exercises

Arrange to see a pupil
  (1) who is finding the work of the class difficult.
  (2) who is persistently troublesome in class.
  (3) with whom you have been unable to make contact.
  (4) who is so tired in class that his work is suffering.
  (5) who is new to your class.
  (6) who is a persistent truant.

Teaching points

1. Short interviews of above nature can be testing and are likely to promote valuable discussion on, for instance, motivation of pupils, disciplinary procedures, teacher-pupil relationships, inter-professional cooperation.

2. Although certain problems have been suggested, choice of problem could in practice well be left to students.

FINAL COMMENTS

The training sessions envisaged throughout this section have been taken to be workshops in which, through the medium of role-play, students have been given an opportunity to grow in understanding of classroom interaction.

Students engaging in the workshops should accept responsibility for their own learning and also recognise the contribution that each can make in assisting others to learn.

The tutor should appreciate the importance of working to achieve and maintain an atmosphere in which students feel sufficiently secure to admit to their own errors of judgement and profit from them.

PART TWO : SECTION TWO

DEVELOPMENT OF CONVERSATIONAL SKILLS

There are three parts in this section. Each part offers suggestions for the use of role-play in the development of skills. Attention will be focused on three areas:

    i pupils in the primary school (p.96)
    ii older pupils (p.104)
    iii less-able pupils (p.119).

Arguments will not be offered on the need to develop conversational ability. Nevertheless, this section is written from the belief that the ability should be developed.

As soon, however, as any person moves into the area of speaking, and more especially into the development of skills, others speculate upon motives and objectives. So it is essential at this stage to define terms, to describe the type of training envisaged, and to look at the problems of encouraging others to develop their own conversational potential.

DEFINITIONS

CONVERSATION

A conversation is social behaviour during the process of which messages pass between participants. People engage in conversation for a variety of reasons. A conservation may last for a few seconds or occupy a considerable period of time. The subject matter may be of little consequence or of extreme importance.

TO COMMUNICATE

The verb *communicate* should be taken to describe the process by which a speaker and one or more listeners make contact with each other through the medium of words, incidental sounds, tone of voice, gestures and other bodily movements. The contacting is a continuing process of interaction—that is, while A is sending out messages to B, A is at the same time receiving messages from B. Communication is effective when the sender of the message becomes aware that it has been received apparently as intended: a failure in communication occurs when there has been misunderstanding of intention or when the message has not registered. Communication is not considered only in terms of resultant co-operative behaviour. If A wishes to insult B and it becomes obvious that this has happened, then although the result may be conflict there has been communication and a conversational objective achieved.

MESSAGE

The information that passes between partners. Messages cannot be transmitted in their original form. Thoughts, feelings, desires, commands, etc., require to be transformed into signals that can be transmitted by one person and perceived by another. Such signals can be classified under two headings (a) verbal (b) non-verbal, both vocal and visual.

In addition to the various signals that are consciously transmitted from person to person, each person may collect information about the other on the evidence of such matters as clothes, hair styles, personal belongings, etc.

CONVERSATIONAL PARTNERS

A conversation presupposes at least two participants—an initiator and a responder. If one considers the initiator to be the speaker, then the responder would be the listener. It is very easy, when trying to assess the contributions which each participant makes in conversation, to focus attention, particularly in the context of training, upon the abilities of the speaker. Indeed speakers frequently take the listener's comprehension for granted, assuming that if thoughts are well marshalled, words carefully chosen, diction clear, and the message given with 'sincerity' then willy-nilly comprehension will follow. This is not so. The listener will grant the speaker just as much attention as seems desirable at the moment and will, of course, impose his own meaning upon the speaker's message. Just as the speaker is a unique individual with his own knowledge, memories and life experiences, all of which influence any contributions which he chooses to make, so the listener's responses are born of his individuality. Listener and speaker are *partners* in conversation, and each is required to take account of the other if communication is to be achieved.

SPEAKING STYLE

The term is synonymous with 'manner of address'. It is an umbrella term covering choice of words, pronunciation, tone of voice, indeed all the verbal and non-verbal signals the speaker employs. Style is considered to be effective or ineffective in relation to the listener, the setting and the circumstances in which the conversation takes place. Some speakers have a range of styles from which they can make the most appropriate choice. For others choice is limited.

COMPETENCE

In some activities it is possible to measure competence. The golfer who does a hole in 4 strokes beats the one who takes 5. The one who returns better figures consistently is the more competent golfer. The motorist who can reverse into a narrow space without touching kerb or other parked cars is more skilled than the one who cannot. The ability to sing in tune is a yardstick that can be applied to singers. But what is the yardstick by which we may assess competence in conversational ability? The closer we look into the problem of trying to do so, the more impossible it is to come up with anything other than a loose statement. To be competent in conversation there must be the ability to sustain, more often than not, co-operative relationships in a wide range of circumstances. The good conversationalist is able to pick up both the verbal and the non-verbal signals; to adjust behaviour on the basis of the messages gained from the signals; and to respond in a manner that the other person(s) will find appropriate. Competence in conversation is therefore seen, not in terms of individual speech and/or language skills, but in individual capacity to use skills in contact with others.

TYPE OF TRAINING ENVISAGED

The type of training in mind is confined to the development of ability to engage in conversation in everyday unspecialised situations that call forth no extraordinary vocal ability. It is not equated with speech or language training nor with the development of a socially acceptable speaking style.

The following distinctions are made:

Speech training is concerned with the speaker's vocal ability and deals with aspects of technique such as variety, breath control, diction, modulation.

Language training focuses attention upon development of vocabulary, grammatical patterns, semantics, etc.

Training towards a more socially acceptable speaking style offers a model and encourages speakers to copy the recommended style.

The above three types of training can all proceed in isolation. Such training prepares people for conversation by developing skills to be used in action with others whether in the role of speaker or listener.

Training in conversation cannot proceed in isolation: the presence of both speaker and listener is necessary to the process. This training is concerned with Interaction, with the use to which participants put their skills in contact with each other.

There is nothing inherently superior or inferior in any one of the above types of training. They are different, they have different objectives, and they are all important in their own context.

OBJECTIVES

What happens when two people meet? They notice each other and consciously or sub-consciously size up each other and the total situation. Taking part in a conversation that will be a satisfactory experience for all conversationalists involves not only the ability to recognise what may be expected of one but also the capacity to meet expectations in verbal and non-verbal terms.

Talking and listening are social activities that require to be practised. Sometimes circumstances in which individuals grow up are not conducive to the practising of skills, and this can result in lack of self-confidence.

The objectives in training are therefore to encourage pupils to become involved in their own learning so that they may:

develop self confidence;
increase knowledge of the reciprocal nature of inter-personal communication;
practise skills;
widen the range of circumstances in which they can operate with comfort.

TRAINING PROBLEMS

The task of encouraging conversational potential is not an easy one. Those who try to do so will often meet with resistance, but if any progress is to be made there has to be understanding of difficulties inherent in the task. So it is important to look in some detail at possible pupil resistance. Begin with the teacher.

A teacher who offers training in conversation is in a peculiar position. In the teaching of subjects such as mathematics, history, art, or physical education, the teacher's knowledge of subject matter is normally apparent even when those being taught fail to respond. However, when training is concerned with the development of communication skills the teacher is in a vulnerable position. If the teacher fails in the exercise of his or her skills with a class or with individual members of it, that teacher is seen to be ineffective in his or her own specialism. Indeed, a teacher, while wishing to help pupils develop their own skills, may in his or her own person be the greatest stumbling block to progress. This claim requires explanation.

Setting aside disability for the time being, it may be assumed that every pupil in a class, has on at least some occasion been able to converse satisfactorily with at least one person. If a pupil at any moment in class finds communication difficult or impossible then at least one feature of the situation is creating problems for that pupil. The sources of any such problems are many and varied, but it may be that the teacher is, because of his or her own speaking style, presenting a major threat to that pupil.

When teacher and pupil fail to get on each other's wave length there is a tendency for the teacher to assess the pupil's speaking style and to point out aspects of it that require attention without at the same time acknowledging the features of his or her own style that are contributing to the joint failure. That both parties have contributed to the failure is undeniable and to suggest to a pupil that he is wrong and the teacher is right does little to encourage potential.

It is not suggested that to be effective in communication with pupils a teacher must adopt their style of speaking. Were that to happen, the ploy would soon be recognised for what it was worth. But interest, care, and intention are communicated more through non-verbal than through verbal signals, so what teachers say *through* their voices and facial expressions is crucial to the breaking down of any barrier which may have been raised by different speaking styles.

Because a teacher is a teacher, however, there will be a desire to open up a choice of speaking styles for pupils so that they may be effective in a wide range of circumstances, but this may prove to be a very difficult task. Take this situation, for example:

Two Scots boys aged thirteen were overheard engaged in the following conversation:

		Standard English equivalent
A.	Goin' t'th' gem?	Going to the game?
B.	Na. Skint. Seeiton Telly.	No. I've no money. See it on TV.
A.	Whi' aboo' Tam?	What about Tom?
B.	He's gaun 'n th' bus.	He's going on the bus.
A.	Be a guid gem three—nil.	Be a good game three—nil.
B.	Na—nae chance.	No—no chance.
A.	Wanna bet?	Want to bet?
B.	Too easy	Too easy

Silence . . .

B.	Heard The Stones' new wan?	Heard The Stones' new one?
A.	Aye. Crap.	Yes. Rubbish.
B.	Ah like it. Be'er than tha' there at nummer wan.	I like it. Better than the one at number one.

Silence . . .

B.	Fag?	Cigarette?
A.	Ta.	Thanks.

Silence . . .

A.	'Sthera Disco th' night?	Is there a Disco tonight?
B.	Dunno.	Don't know.

In that conversation communication was achieved. The boys exchanged messages to each other's satisfaction. In different circumstances with a different conversational partner each boy might well have been at some disadvantage.

So the teacher has a problem and a complex one, for he must try to help each individual pupil to widen his or her range while at the same time being careful not to say or do anything that will diminish a pupil's self esteem.

This is a major problem for there is a long history of suspicion and scepticism attached to any training associated with speaking.

Few will risk their reputations by becoming involved in training which they may consider unnecessary, irrelevant, unworthy of serious attention, or a comment on their personality and social background. In addition, pupils may be experiencing no difficulty in conversing with others except in school, and therefore they may have no sense of loss. Paradoxically, however, pupils may attach considerable importance to the ability to converse even if they are not prepared to acknowledge such thoughts.

Tutors have to deal in their own way with the problem of encouraging pupils to become involved in their own learning. Adverse criticism of the way a pupil speaks can lead to a serious loss of confidence which may be felt by that pupil well into adulthood. Tutors may find that role-play helps to motivate pupils, so how can it be used for this purpose?

i CONVERSATION IN PRIMARY SCHOOL

EARLY CLASSES OF THE PRIMARY SCHOOL

At what age should you introduce role-play into training? Obviously one would not use role-play for analytical purposes in the early classes of primary school, nor should the technique be used in a formal way at that level. But, as already noted in Part I, children engage in their own form of role-play and so the teacher will have opportunity to take part in their play to the advantage of all concerned.

Coming to school for the first time, children are entering a strange world. Children who live in families where conversational opportunities are limited are particularly disadvantaged. A major task of the teacher is to enable each child to develop speech and language skills. As a consequence, the kind of conversational training envisaged for older pupils is not appropriate for the 5–8 age range. Nevertheless, indirectly, the teacher can do much to lay the foundation for competence in face-to-face interaction.

In the modern primary school, children develop mentally, emotionally and socially through participation in play activities. On many occasions the teacher will remain outside the play but there will be opportunities for her to enter into the child's play world, become part of it and stimulate learning from within. The following account of such an occasion illustrates what is meant.

When talking to a small group of boys in Primary 1, a teacher was approached by one of the girls.

'Would you like to visit our hospital?'

'Thank you very much, I'd love to.'

The teacher made her excuses to the boys and followed the child up to a corner of the room where, behind a screen, two dolls were tucked up in two little beds. Beside the beds were two little girls dressed as nurses and one little boy in his outdoor coat (he was a parent visiting his sick child). The teacher, now in the role of hospital visitor, opened the conversation:

VISITOR: Good morning! I have come to visit your hospital. Who is Matron?

MATRON: I am matron.

VISITOR: Good morning, matron, and how are your patients this morning?

MATRON: Getting on very nicely, thank you.

This visit lasted about five minutes during which time the visitor heard all about the patients and was given a cup of tea. After an exchange of farewells, the visitor left the hospital.

It is important to note the role-change. As a 'visitor' the teacher went into the hospital and, merely by playing that role in relation to the roles the children had assumed, provided opportunity for learning. Once the teacher adopts her role she must play it through to the end of the situation. It would lead to confusion and lack of confidence were she to change back to 'teacher' while in the situation either to criticise or to control the behaviour of pupils. If the latter became necessary she would require to do so in terms of her assumed role.

At this stage in development children are encountering language and it is particularly important that they are given opportunity to develop confidence in the use of words. The process by which pupils learn to use words appropriate to circumstances can be helped through the teacher playing an active part in the role-play of her pupils. This, of course, is work with which all primary teachers will be familiar and one has only to mention shopping, telephone conversations, tea-parties, to appreciate the extent to which simulation is used to facilitate learning.

Children who come to school from homes where conversation is limited will have, in addition to a poor vocabulary, little skill in the social activity. To take part in a conversation one must have something to say, words in which to say it, and the desire to do so. If a child is not in the habit of speaking he is likely to experience some difficulty in the process of acquiring the habit. Such children need very special care and attention.

Role-play with young children, then, proceeds on two levels. While the children are engaged on their level, quite unconscious of any educational value, the teacher is operating quite consciously on hers, observing her pupils and prepared to enter into their play when it is considered appropriate to do so.

As the child moves up the school his control over his speech mechanism becomes more secure and his vocabulary enlarges. At the same time he becomes more aware of the positive part the listener plays in the communication process. He begins to learn that it is necessary to adapt his speaking to meet the expectations of listeners in each and every situation. He comes to realise that if he misjudges a situation then the consequences may well be uncomfortable. For example, if he confuses the playground with his home and his mother with a friend he may suffer the consequences if in words selected and manner of utterance he has made a poor choice.

It is at this stage in the child's development that the adult technique can be introduced into training.

SENIOR PUPILS IN A PRIMARY SCHOOL

Perhaps the best way to introduce ideas for exercises with senior pupils is to give an account of work done with a particular class of pupils in a school in Edinburgh. The work was undertaken with pupils who had no particular difficulties with speech or language and for whom talking presented no serious problems. These exercises would not necessarily be suitable for other groups of pupils. Exercises should meet the needs of specific pupils and be relevant in the context of their own circumstances.

EXERCISE A

Training objectives were:

    (1) to introduce pupils to the technique of role-play

    (2) to stimulate thinking about everyday conversations.

Class: Primary 7 boys and girls.

Teacher's brief to the class

Today we are going to experiment. I would like you all to think of your-selves leaving school at 3.30 p.m. You are chatting to your friends. Most of you go straight home. Some of the boys, however, hang around the playground kicking a ball about. One of those boys suddenly remembers that he has to be home by four o'clock. He hasn't a watch and needs to know the time. Got the picture?

Kenneth, you be the boy who wants to know the time. Stephen, you are playing football. By the way, Kenneth, why have you to be home by 4.00 p.m.?

KENNETH: Mother wants me to do some shopping for her.

TEACHER: Fine, we will take up the situation at the moment when Kenneth remembers about the shopping, stops playing football and decides to ask Stephen the time. Is everything clear?

JACK: Have we to play football?

TEACHER: I think that would be a little difficult in the classroom. Let's say that you have just stopped playing.

I would like the rest of the class to look and listen.

Playing/Observing

KENNETH (*shouting over to Stephen*): Hi—Stephen?

STEPHEN (*shouting back to Kenneth*): What?

KENNETH: What's the time?

STEPHEN: Couldn't tell you—I've not got my watch on.

KENNETH: Right thanks, Cheerio.

STEPHEN: Cheerio.

TEACHER: Not having had any success with Stephen, Kenneth sees his headmaster coming out of school and decides to ask him. Tom, will you be the headmaster? Will everyone watch and this time try to notice in what ways this new conversation differs from the last one.

Playing/Observing

KENNETH (*approaching the headmaster and in a quiet voice*): Excuse me please, sir, do you have the time?

HEADMASTER: Oh yes, Kenneth. It's ten to four.

KENNETH: Thank you very much, sir. Goodbye.

HEADMASTER: Cheerio.

TEACHER: That was good. I wonder if we could try another conversation. Do you think there would be any difference in the way Kenneth spoke if he were addressing one of the overseas students? Margaret, you be a student. Where do you come from?

STUDENT: From Africa.

TEACHER: And how long have you been in Edinburgh?

STUDENT: Just two months.

TEACHER: Thank you. Everybody ready?

Playing/Observing

KENNETH (*approaching the student*): Excuse me, please, do you have the time?

STUDENT: Time? The Time?

KENNETH: Yes, the hour.

STUDENT: Oh yes, it is nearly four o'clock.

KENNETH: Oh, thank you. Thank you very much.

STUDENT: Thank you too.

TEACHER: That was most interesting. Observers, what are some of the things that you noticed?

REPLIES: When Kenneth spoke to the headmaster he spoke very courteously.

When he spoke to the overseas students he had to speak distinctly.

TEACHER: Why?

REPLIES: Because she didn't understand the language very well.

She didn't know much English.

TEACHER: Did any of you notice the words Kenneth used to ask the time? He said to the student 'Do you have the time?' He said that to the headmaster but the headmaster knew that Kenneth was really saying 'Will you tell me the time?' Foreigners may not understand the phrase 'Do you have the time?' It is a colloquialism and when it was used with the student it led to some confusion. But let us turn to the Kenneth/Stephen conversation. What did you notice?

REPLIES: Kenneth and Stephen shouted at each other.

Kenneth wasn't worried about how he spoke.

He was more casual.

TEACHER: Much more casual. What about words?

REPLIES: Kenneth said Hi to his friend and Cheerio.

He used more chummy words.

TEACHER: All right, Kenneth, could you sum up for us what we have discovered?

KENNETH: You can shout to your friends but to people you respect you should speak far more courteously. If you are speaking to a foreigner you must take time to speak more clearly and try to use words she will understand.

TEACHER: Well done.

EXERCISE B

TUTOR: We have already discovered that we do not speak in the same way to everyone that we meet. The words we choose to use, the way we speak

these words and the tone of voice all vary according to the particular
person we are addressing. Today, we shall carry out a further experiment
to find out some other things about speaking. This is a sad tale of a lost
purse.

Brief: Mrs Smith sent her daughter, Betty, down to the shops. Betty goes
into the grocers, gets what she wants. When the shopkeeper tells her what
the goods all come to, Betty feels for her purse and discovers it's not there.
She goes home, tells her mother, who sends her to the police station. On
the way there she meets two friends. She arrives at the police station and
the story ends when Betty leaves the station.

We will need Betty, her mother, two school friends, a shopkeeper, and a
police officer.

(Roles are allocated).

Each of you will need to make up your minds about yourselves. For
instance, Mrs Smith, are you well-off? Betty, decide whether or not you
knew the exact amount of money that was in your purse when you lost it.
Shopkeeper—is Betty a regular customer? Decide between you. While you
are all thinking about your roles I'll talk to the others.

Observers are divided into four groups.

Group A, you concentrate on the shopkeeper conversation.
Group B, concentrate on the Betty/Mother conversation.
Group C, on Betty with her friends.
Group D, you pay partictular attention to the conversation in the police
station.

We will start in the grocer's shop at the moment when Betty has asked for
all she wants.

Interaction

SHOPKEEPER: Is that all?
BETTY: Yes, how much is that, please?
SHOPKEEPER: One pound, forty pence.
BETTY *(Betty feels for her purse and begins to look worried.):* I can't find my
purse.
SHOPKEEPER: Maybe it's in your other pocket. Have another look.
BETTY: No, its not there.
SHOPKEEPER: You'll have dropped it on the floor.
BETTY: No, I can't see it.
SHOPKEEPER: How much was in it?
BETTY: Three pounds.

SHOPKEEPER: What will your mother say?

BETTY: I don't know. She'll be angry.

SHOPKEEPER: I'll tell you what I'll do, I'll take a note of the amount and you can hand it in later. Don't worry now. Just tell your mother what happened. She'll go to the police and maybe they'll have it.

TUTOR: And now Betty, you go home to tell your mother and this is Group B's Conversation.

BETTY: Mum, I've got something to tell you.

MUM: What is it, dear?

BETTY: I've lost my purse.

MUM: Oh how did you do that?

BETTY: It must have slipped out of my pocket.

MUM: Now where were you?

BETTY: I went to the chemist's.

MUM: Do you think you left it there?

BETTY: No, because I paid him and I remember putting my purse back into my pocket.

MUM: What streets did you go down?

BETTY: Keil Street and Station Road.

MUM: So you might have lost it in either of these two. Well, off you go to the police station. You have been very careless. Be sure to tell them everything.

TUTOR: On the way to the station you meet two friends.

BETTY: Hiya Kenny. Hiya Chick. Listen I've lost my purse.

CHICK: How much was in it?

BETTY: Three quid.

KENNY: Gee—where did you lose it?

BETTY: I don't know, maybe in Keil Street or Station Road.

CHICK: Come on. We'll help you to look for it.

BETTY: No, I've got to go to the police station.

KENNY: We'll go and have a look anyway.

BETTY: Thanks. Cheerio.

TUTOR: And so you arrive at the police station.

BETTY: Excuse me please. I've lost my purse.

P.O.: We'll have to look into this. What was the colour?

BETTY: Blue.

P.O.: Size? Was it a big purse or small one?

BETTY: Quite small.

P.O.: Was it a leather purse?

BETTY: Yes.
P.O.: What's your name?
BETTY: Betty Smith.
P.O.: Where do you live?
BETTY: 3a Ivy Street.
P.O.: How much was in the purse?
BETTY: Three pounds.
P.O.: Now off you go home. If we get any word of it we'll let you know. Right?

TUTOR: There we had six people all involved in one way or another with the problem of the lost purse. There were four different conversations. What did you notice?
GROUP A: The shopkeeper wanted her money. She was sorry for Betty and helped her to look for her purse. She sympathised with Betty.
TUTOR: How did you know she was sorry for her? What told you she was sorry for her? Because she didn't say, 'I'm sorry for you, Betty '.
GROUP A: It was her voice and her face. She looked sorry and she sounded sorry. Betty looked upset when she couldn't find her purse. I thought she was going to cry.
GROUP B: Mrs Smith was very angry. She looked very angry and she sounded angry. She thought Betty had been careless and that made her angry. She wanted her money back. That was what she was wanting and so she sent Betty to the police station.
GROUP C: Chick and Kenny wanted to help Betty. It was just the friendship with them. Betty couldn't wait because she had to go to the police. She didn't really have time to speak to them.
GROUP D: The policeman was interested in the purse. Where Betty had lost it. What size it was, and what colour. He wanted to know how much was in the purse. The policeman was abrupt.
TEACHER: What do you mean by abrupt?
GROUP D: He spoke in short sentences like—'What colour was it? and 'What's your name?'
TUTOR: Why do you think he spoke like that? Policeman, you tell us.
POLICEMAN: I wanted to get the purse back. I needed to know what it looked like.
TEACHER: Betty, what were you thinking about?
BETTY: I got a fright when I couldn't find my purse. I knew my mother would be angry. I was upset. I didn't have the time to look for it with Kenny and Chick. I didn't like going to the police station.
TEACHER: Some of you said Mrs Smith was very angry, then someone else said she looked angry and she sounded angry. So we do tell people what we are thinking and feeling, and not just through words.

The discussion continued. The exercises were useful in that pupils were introduced to role-play They enjoyed the experience and their thinking about conversation was stimulated.

The plan, now, is to suggest role-play exercises that might be used in teaching programmes designed to increase knowledge of inter-personal communication and to promote greater confidence in talking. Sets of exercises are offered for use with (a) older pupils, (b) less able pupils.

Introductory comments precede each set of exercises and such observations represent build-up talk that a teacher might give at the start of a lesson. Although each role-play will provide its own material for discussion, some of the points that might well be revealed during the role-play of a suggested exercise are anticipated. At other times, attention is directed to some important issues. It is assumed that the given situations will be adapted and briefing filled out to meet the requirements of a particular class.

ii CONVERSATION FOR OLDER PUPILS

In what circumstances do you find it easy to take part in a conversation?
Do you ever refrain from speaking to protect yourself from possible reactions
   to your voice or your comments?
Do you know what it feels like to be lost for words?
Does the role of listener come easier to you than that of speaker?

These questions have been posed to focus attention on feelings and therefore upon major reasons why people can find talking an uncomfortable experience.

It is only natural that certain types of conversation should induce anxiety or bring little enjoyment, but many people experience discomfort on too many occasions and therefore fail to make the best of themselves in company. It may be that those adults who feel discomfort or are inhibited in conversation have had little opportunity to converse with others outside family or friendship circles. It may be that when they were young too much emphasis was placed on the acquisition of speech and language skills and on 'correct' pronunciation.

Adverse criticism is inhibiting and at no time more so than in the years of adolescence. With older pupils, training for the development of conversational skills should be concerned primarily with the building up of confidence. This is best achieved through work which the pupils are likely to find interesting and, above all, enjoyable. If pupils begin to associate talking with pleasure they may then wish to become more skilled and more knowledgeable.

As a first stage in training, exercises should be chosen for their entertainment value. Once interest is captured and pupils begin to enjoy their work, exercises to increase understanding of and skill in inter-personal communication may be introduced. Exercises are therefore, grouped into separate sets. It is suggested that exercises should be chosen from the first set before any from the second set are given, unless, of course, particular pupils are already comfortable in conversation.

FIRST SET

Theme: Enjoyment

Exercises are not given in any special order.

(1) Get sheets of paper equal to number of pupils and tutor. Head each sheet with a relevant question. Shuffle papers and give one sheet to each pupil—tutor keeping one. Explain to pupils that they should put their given questions to ten pupils and record each reply. When, for example, Pupil A puts her question to pupil B and has written down the reply, pupil B should question pupil A before they part. Explain, also that names are not to be recorded. Each reply is to be numbered.

Teaching points

The tutor takes part on the same basis as pupils. Questions should be centred round out-of-school experiences and interests.

The exercise provides pupils with words to say, i.e. the written question and a reason for speaking. By the end of the exercise all will have spoken to ten different people—among whose number, for some, will have been the tutor.

(2) Operate in groups of eight or so. Cut up eight slips of paper (2×2 in). Leave seven slips blank and fold twice. Put the letter L on the remaining slip and fold. Explain to pupils that all slips save one are blank, and that the one slip bears the letter L. Ask the eight pupils to draw a slip but to keep it folded meantime.

Explain the game which is—pupils in turn are required to talk about something that happened to them. All must tell the truth except the pupil who has drawn the 'L' slip. He must lie.

When everyone is clear about the game, pupils may look at their slips, trying not to indicate whether they have drawn the Liar slip or not.

The stories are told.

Thereafter each pupil should say who he thinks is the liar and of course the liar would also choose someone. At the end the liar declares himself or herself.

Teaching point

Although overtly this game is concerned with talking, it will be found that the concentration of listeners is keener than is normal.

(3) Pre-arrange with three or four pupils to prepare a small dramatic scene which must follow an agreed sequence of actions. This will be enacted in front of the remainder of the class. On completion the actors go behind classmates—out of sight—while pupils are asked not to look round at them.

Either the tutor, or a fifth pupil who has had advance notice, then announces that he is a police officer and everyone has witnessed the incident. He requires to find out what exactly transpired. The police officer then questions the group to establish appearance, sequence of action, etc. etc. When this has been completed the actors come back into focus and comparisons are made.

Teaching points

It is essential that the actors follow exactly the pre-arranged sequence of behaviour. This should be known to the tutor. If the exercise raises questions on selective perception, identity parades, etc, the tutor should encourage conversation on these matters.

In Section 1, under the heading Observation, other exercises were explained: these might well be considered suitable also for older pupils.

(4) Equipment required: tape and microphone
    Roles: sales representative; customers

Preparation: The tutor should prepare a story for the sale of a particular product. For instance, the story might begin along the following lines, 'I am sales representative for the Firm SAFE AND SURE and I would like to interest you in a very special product that has just come on to the market'. Here would follow details of the product and advantages for the purchaser.

Method: Ask a certain number of pupils to leave the room—possibly six. Set the tape recorder in position and place the microphone on a table. Arrange one chair behind the table and one in front. Sit in the chair behind the table. Ask a pupil to bring in the first customer. Go through the sales talk. This should be recorded, with a pupil operating the recorder.

At the end of the tale the recorder is stopped and the pupil who has been the customer takes over the role of sales representative. The second pupil is brought into the room. The new sales representative, using information that he or she remembers, sells the product to the new customer. The sales talk is recorded. When the final customer has heard the sales talk he then becomes the sales representative and gives his sales talk to the tutor who started it all. The tape is then played back.

Teaching points

It should be interesting to hear what pieces of information survived accurately; what distortions, additions, etc., were introduced en route.

(5) Equipment: One suitcase containing items not normally found in a case.
    Roles: Customs Officer, and travellers
Method: Ask a certain number of pupils to leave the room. One by one they enter the room to be confronted by the Customs Officer and their (supposedly) own suitcase. Each traveller is required to explain contents.

(6) Introduce this exercise by saying something like, 'You all need a photograph, maybe for some sports programme or magazine, and you have asked me to take your photo. Before doing so, I shall need certain information'.
    Give out sheets of paper. Ask each pupil to record answers to questions of the following nature:

Location—where is the photo to be taken—indoors, outdoors, where?
Clothes—what do you wish to wear?
Posture—how much of yourself is to be photographed—full length, head and shoulders only, waist up? Do you want to sit, stand, lie, kneel?
Anything else to be included in your photo?
If your hands are seen, are they touching or holding anything, and if so what?
Do you wish anyone else to be in the photograph. If so, who?
What expression is to be on your face?
What should people who see your photograph take from the expression in your eyes?
How often do you look as you have described?
Would people who know you be surprised if they saw this photograph?

After answering the questions the pupils may talk about their photographs to each other, and to the tutor.

Teaching points

Most people are really quite interested in themselves. This exercise gives pupils an opportunity to build up a picture of themselves and then have the pleasure of laughing about it with others. The exercise therefore has the great advantage of providing something to talk about: it can be a most useful one with pupils who need to be encouraged to talk.

Like most of the exercises this one can be entertaining on the surface but can give rise to conversation at a deeper level.

(7) *Profiles.* This is another 'lever' exercise. It contributes to an opening process that helps pupils to say what they have in mind, and perhaps at the same time it provides an opportunity for the better understanding of relationships.

Preparation: Choose two contrasting roles e.g. student/apprentice; athlete/ artist; employer/employee. Write a different comment on ten cards. Write the same comments on another set of ten cards. Use a different colour for the duplicate set.

Sample comments: 'Has a responsible attitude to work', 'Is a good time-keeper', 'Makes a worthwhile contribution to society'.

(Comments should be relevant in terms of chosen contrasting roles).

Organise a Board as illustrated.

EMPLOYEE			EMPLOYER		
YES		NO	YES		NO

Explain to the class that profiles will be built up according to their specifications. Take each pair of cards in turn. Read the written comment to pupils. Ask pupils where cards should be placed. Place each card in the Yes or No columns according to instructions from pupils. If the response to what is written is 'Don't know' or 'It depends', place the card in the space between the Yes and No columns.

Example. Chosen roles: employer/employee.

A set of blue cards is prepared for employer and a set of red ones for employee. One pair of cards carries the comment 'Has a responsible attitude towards work'. The comment on the blue card is read to pupils. If they consider that employers have a responsible attitude towards work they instruct the tutor to place the card in the employer's Yes column. If they are of the contrary opinion the card goes in the No column. If opinion is divided or there is a measure of doubt, the card is placed in the neutral area between the two positive columns. The red card, i.e. the employee card bearing the same comment, is then dealt with similarly. Repeat until all cards are on the board. Consider implications with pupils.

(8) *Diagrams.* Draw a diagram on a sheet of paper. This should consist of lines, circles, squares, etc., and be geometric, not representational. Ask one pupil to sit out in front of the class. Give the diagram to this pupil. Issue one sheet of the same size paper to each pupil.

The exercise is in two parts.

A. The pupil who has the sheet of paper bearing the diagram is required to describe what is in front of her in verbal terms only. No gestures may be used and the diagram may not be shown to the class nor drawn on a blackboard. Pupils are required to draw on their own piece of paper according to the instructions given to them. They may not ask for additional information, clarification or repetition. They may not consult neighbours. After the diagram has been fully described, the versions that pupils have drawn are compared with the original. There will be considerable variation in the drawings and some, at least, will bear little resemblance to the original.

B. Have a second diagram prepared and give this to a second pupil to describe. The first pupil takes part in the repeat exercise—as a member of the class. This time, however, although the same restrictions are placed upon the describer, pupils may ask for clarification or for additional information and may ask the describer to repeat his instructions.

On completion, compare the drawings. These will be much closer to the original than was the case in the first part of the exercise.

Discuss implications.

Teaching points

This exercise provides an excellent introduction into inter-personal communication, in that it highlights the reciprocal nature of communication; it draws attention to the verbal and non-verbal elements that coexist in conversation; and it emphasises the importance of the speaker and the listener each being on the other's wavelength. An exercise such as this could therefore easily lead on to the second set of exercises which are designed to develop skills and extend knowledge.

SECOND SET

Themes: Extension of knowledge
          Development of skills.
Several aspects of inter-personal communication might have engaged attention but four are selected to illustrate how role-play may be used to advance learning: nature of speech, conversational partners, conversational functions and conversational occasions.

   This is not intended to be a scheme of work but only an illustration of how role-play could be used in a scheme of work designed to promote conversational potential.

NATURE OF SPEECH

People are apt to think that when they speak they are just voicing words, but when people talk they make sounds that are non-verbal. In conversation, most people use 'ums', and 'ahs' and throat-clearing noises. In addition there are accompanying visual signals—that exist in speech but are not recorded when speech is converted to written language. There is a tendency also for people to think that they always pronounce words in the same way. In fact, if they really listen to themselves they must hear that they do not.
'Good Morning!' Readers will no doubt pronounce these words giving each their full value but if the words are said to a friend in a familiar setting then their pronunciation would be different. 'Good' would be very weakly articulated and 'morning' would sound like—let pupils try it. Do some of the sounds disappear? The greeting may be understood because of the tone of voice, the head nod, or the circumstances in which it is being spoken. In other circumstances, of course, both words may be given their full sound value.

   The first exercises should be designed, therefore, to help pupils appreciate the nature of speech.

   Pupils should be asked to identify categories of persons who use signs as a means of conveying information to others. Lists might include: points duty policeman, hockey umpire, persons who are deaf, tipster at a racecourse, lollipop lady.

   In the ordinary business of living, human beings use certain gestures instead of words to convey intention. Examples may be sought from pupils: e.g. Thumb up, thumb down, finger across lip with lips closed, beckoning finger, shake of head from side to side, nod of head.

Pupils should be asked to what extent do people use gestures when they talk with each other?

A television programme without the sound may be shown and pupils' observations sought. Pupils should be asked to notice, on the way home and coming back to school, the different gestures people make when chatting to each other. At the next meeting of the class pupils should report their observations. To reinforce learning and to help pupils appreciate the extent to which they depend upon non-verbal signals in conversation, the role-play exercises outlined in section 1 in the area of inter-personal communication may be used.

When it is established that speech is not only the utterance of words but also the accompanying facial expressions and general movements of the body, pupils should be led to appreciate the flexibility that exists in the pronunciation of words and the significance of vocal tone.

A tape recording should be prepared in which persons engage in telephone conversations. For instance:

1(a) A person making an appointment with a hairdresser—dentist or similar.
  (b) The same person making an appointment to meet a friend.
2(a) A person seeking information from some organisation e.g. British Rail.
  (b) The same person seeking information from a neighbour.
3(a) A person phoning a friend to say that he has a sprained ankle and will not be at the club tonight.
  (b) The same person phoning his boss to say he has a sprained ankle and will not be in to work.

The first pair of conversations is played back. Pupils are asked to note and comment on the tone of voice and the pronunciation of words in both conversations. The conversations are re-played to give pupils an opportunity to check their observations.

The second tape is played. Attention is directed to the caller and pupils are asked to say in what specific ways vocal behaviour was different in the two conversations.

When the final pair is played, pupils are asked to focus on the response of the friend and of the boss to the news. What interested them? How is this revealed? Pupils should be advised to listen to talk on radio and television and to note the incidence of non-verbal signals both vocal and visual.

Teaching points

Role-play should help pupils to appreciate that speech is different from written language and is not a sound equivalent.

Exercises might lead pupils into discussing attitude to accents, their own prejudices, and the extent to which they make judgements about people on the basis of their speaking habits.

In addition, pupils may be asked to consider the effect that the vocal behaviour of, for instance, political leaders, public speakers, television advertisements has upon listeners.

CONVERSATIONAL PARTNERS

Those who engage in conversation, whether in the role of speaker or listener, are partners. It takes at least two people to make conversation. Is this true or false? Must there be cooperation? Just how dependent is each upon the other? For the first three exercises pupils work in buzz groups simultaneously.

First Exercise

A, B and C in each buzz group are friends. The A in each group is asked to think of something he or she would like to tell B and C.

The As are given individual briefing: you must not use English to convey message; you may use any foreign language or make up your own nonsense words; you may make full use of facial expressions and gestures.

Interaction

Second Exercise

In this role-play the Bs have a message to convey to others.

The Bs are given individual briefing: You have lost your voice and must try to get your message over to A and C by means of facial expressions and gestures only; you may not write anything down; you can indicate that you have lost your voice by means of gestures.

Interaction

Third Exercise

Cs are briefed: Think of something you want to tell A and B.

As and Bs are given independent briefing: Each of you think of something you want to tell C; don't tell each other what it is and don't tell C what you have been asked to do, but as soon as C starts to speak each of you proceed to try to get your message across at the same time.

Interaction

In all probability pupils will need time to talk over buzz group experiences in between exercises. In such discussions there is good learning.

Fourth Exercise

This exercise is concerned with words—choice of words, and in particular slang and swear words. Tutor and class discuss: choice of words; the emotive quality of words; the different values people place upon words; the use of words that others would call slang or swearing.

The class is divided into four units. Each unit is given a different task. For instance.

Unit A.   Devise a situation that will demonstrate how the use of words by one or two individuals antagonises the others.

Unit B.   Devise a situation to demonstrate control in the choice of words when a group of young people are joined by an older person.

Unit C.   Devise a situation in which one person objects to the words that others use and is mocked for doing so.

Unit D.   Devise contrasting situations showing differences in choice of words because of different circumstances.

Role-plays proceed in turn with those not engaged in Interaction observing. At their conclusion, discussion is encouraged.

Teaching points

The attempt in this exercise should be to help pupils appreciate words and their suitability in relation to occasion and personnel. There has to be a freedom from humbug in the conduct of such experiences. Pupils and adults do swear and use slang words in conversation. That is fact. Interest here lies in what does happen, what might be avoided, and what could be the consequences if not avoided.

Fifth Exercise

This exercise is also concerned with words—technical terms. A tape is prepared in which there are three or four recorded examples of people using technical terms. For instance: an extract from a cricket commentary; two people discussing the medical history of a patient; instruction on sewing; a talk on car maintenance.

The intention is to demonstrate that where there is no knowledge of terms used there is little understanding of content.

The tape is played in class. The pupils are asked for reactions to each recording. Pupils are asked to consider circumstances in which the use of technical terms by a person in authority causes the recipient of the information to be confused. Some of their suggestions should be role-played, and implications should be discussed.

The final two exercises centre round willingness or capacity to engage in conversation.

Sixth Exercise

The class is divided into two or three units. Each unit is asked to choose a topic of conversation. Three or four are called up from each unit.

Brief: None of you are willing to talk, you want to listen only. If asked a direct question you should answer it non-verbally.

Unit conversations begin when these pupils re-join their own unit. Time is allowed for discussion in units.

General discussion. The units are asked for observations. Pupils are encouraged to comment on reasons why people sometimes prefer to remain silent. Did some of the silent operators find it difficult to keep quiet in the role-play? Reticence, and the feelings of the reticent person when urged to speak, should be considered. Is the ready talker necessarily the most interesting contributor?

Seventh Exercise

Still in units. In each unit there will be three or four persons who are deaf. Each unit chooses another topic of conversation. A different three or four from each unit are called up. Each is given ear plugs and asked to place them in ears before returning to unit. While those who are simulating deafness fix in the ear plugs, the remainder are briefed: You know that you are being joined by persons who are deaf; when they arrive, engage in conversation on your chosen topic and try to include everyone.

At the conclusion of the exercise those who were 'deaf' are asked to describe their feelings and to make observations on the behaviour of the others in their unit.

General discussion. The experiences of the pupils in their unit conversations are recounted. Disability is discussed. What must it be like if you cannot hear too easily and people are laughing and chatting around you? What must it be like to be blind and not to see people talking? What are the problems in the realm of inter-personal communication that come with disability? What is the responsibility of the able towards the disabled?

With the completion of exercises on the theme Conversational Partners, and remembering the statement made at the outset that it takes at least two people to make conversation, pupils should be asked to reflect upon the work they have done, and to summarise what they have learned.

Observations may well include:

(1) a common language is necessary before conversation can proceed;
(2) facial expressions and gestures on their own have limited use only;
(3) people must be prepared to listen to others if there is to be any purposeful communication;
(4) when people do not understand words that others use there is little appreciation of intention and perhaps an increase in tension;
(5) people have different reasons for speaking and sometimes they can speak 'at' rather than 'with' others;
(6) the tone of voice that a speaker uses affects the response of the listener;
(7) people must have the capacity to hear words if a normal conversation is to take place;
(8) no one can make anyone listen to what is being said;
(9) it is easy to become irritated by people who do not seem to understand what you say to them;
(10) it is not so easy to understand the problems that listeners have and it can be difficult to adjust one's own speaking to suit;
(11) quite often more is said by the accompanying facial expressions and gestures than by words;
(12) if all concerned are to benefit from and find satisfaction in a conversation, each must try to take account of the others and seek to engage in an inter-meshing process.

CONVERSATIONAL FUNCTIONS

Why do people talk with each other—for what purposes?

Consider with the class some of the reasons why people do engage in conversations, e.g. to pass the time of day; to ask for something; to gossip; to give information; to complain; to amuse; to persuade; to instruct; to preach.

Talk about differences.

Focus upon short conversations, for instance: If A says 'Hi' what would you expect B to say in reply?. If B says 'Nice day, isn't it' would you expect A to reply with 'Yes, it's 19°C but the weather forecast says it will turn to showers later on in the day?'

Discuss 'passing-the-time-of-day' conversations and their predictability. Consider the use of small talk in other circumstances. Illustrate through role-play.

For example:

Situation: In a bus. Roles: Conductor; traveller.

CONDUCTOR: Fares, please.

TRAVELLER: One to James Street and please could you let me know when to get off?

CONDUCTOR: If you watch out for the station on your left—it's the stop after that. I'll give you a call.

TRAVELLER: Thanks.

CONDUCTOR: Fares please.

TRAVELLER: I'm a stranger to this town. I'm going to visit my niece. She's just newly married and . . .

CONDUCTOR (*mildly impatient*): That's very nice but I've got a full bus so where do you want to go?

TRAVELLER: Sorry, James Street and I don't know when to get off.

CONDUCTOR: I'll shout it out when we get there.

Consider: Are there occasions when the use of small talk eases situations? Are there some occasions when small talk is inappropriate, even irritating? What then, are some of the reasons why people do engage in small talk?

First Exercise

Brief. Work in pairs. Each pair should devise a situation when (*a*) small talk is appropriate and another one (*b*) when it would not be so. Set your situations anywhere: office; store; hairdressers; at home; in school. You do not need to set both conversations in the same place. Role-plays proceed simultaneously.

Second Exercise

Brief. Still work in pairs. Think up a situation in which two people engage in conversation when the purpose is of greater consequence than merely passing the time of day.

For example: a boy tries to persuade his mother to allow him to go somewhere
> a girl tells her friend about some recent experience;
> parents talk about holiday plans;
> a woman goes to see her neighbour to ask for advice.

Take time to decide and set up your own exercise. Begin when ready.

Consider with class: differences between small talk and other conversations. Pose the question: Did any of the pairs use small talk to get the more important questions started?

Third Exercise

Divide class into small units of six or seven pupils.

Brief: Each unit will be given a specific conversational function—the As to persuade, Bs to inform, Cs to describe, Ds to complain. Each unit should then devise a situation in which their conversation will take place. In all of the conversations the people taking part are friends of the same age.

The tutor may require to give examples of suitable situations, for instance:

To persuade: Friends meet to go over the final plans for something they have
all agreed to do together. Just when all arrangements have been made
one of the friends suddenly thinks of a better idea and tries to persuade
the others to change their minds.

To inform: Friends regularly spend some time helping house-bound people
in the community. One of them has just heard of a certain old person
who requires some task performed. He gives out information regarding
the old person and the job to be done.

To describe: Friends meet. One of them has done something or been somewhere different in which the others have not shared. He tells them
about the experience.

To complain: Friends have just arranged to do something on the previous
Saturday. They agreed to meet at a certain place at 10.00 a.m., each to
bring certain articles. One of the number failed to turn up. They all
waited until 10.30 and then set off without him. Two or three days later
the friends are chatting together when the 'missing one' appears and
joins them.

Give time for units to conduct own briefing. In turn listen to conversations.
Encourage units to observe when not engaged in Interaction. Perhaps direct
attention to matters such as: non-verbal contributions; changes in general
atmosphere. Encourage pupils to report what transpired in their own conversations and to make comments on what they observed.

Fourth Exercise

Brief. Introduce other factors into the above situations and try to discover what,
if any, difference these make to the Interaction. Here are the revised briefs:

To persuade: Representatives from different organisations meet together to
go over the final plans for something they have been asked to do
together (for example—visiting a possible camp site). Just when all
arrangements have been made one of the number tries to persuade the
others to change their minds about doing the allocated task.

To inform: Friends regularly spend some time helping house-bound people
in the community. A new member has joined the group for the first time.
After he has been introduced to the others he tells them about an old
person he knows and gives details of the work that needs to be done for her.

To describe: All are members of a particular school or organisation. They are
meeting under the leadership of an adult. One of the number has been
on some visit or engaged in some project. The leader asks that member
to describe experiences.

5

To complain: Friends have arranged to do something on the previous Saturday. They agreed to meet at a certain place at 10.00 a.m., one of them to get the tickets for the particular match/concert to which they were all journeying. He did not turn up. They waited hoping to catch a later bus but still he did not appear. Two or three days later friends are chatting when the 'missing one' appears and joins them.

Give time for unit briefing. Listen to conversations in turn. On completion ask each unit to discuss among themselves to what extent their behaviour was affected by the new factors and in what ways. Ask each unit to report findings.

Draw attention to the reciprocal nature of inter-personal communication and encourage pupils to consider how much they need to take account of the feelings of others when in conversation if they are seeking their cooperation.

CONVERSATIONAL OCCASIONS

Pupils should now be aware that how they speak varies according to objectives, pair-roles and circumstances and these variations are manifest in the choice of words, pronunciation of words, tone of voice, facial expressions and other bodily movements.

The exercises outlined below are not chosen to impress these points upon pupils but rather to provide them with opportunities to discover the truth of them for themselves as they engage in the different role-plays. When considering suitable exercises the aim should be to choose ones that will stimulate pupils to give of their best.

From the following suggestions, tutors should find some that are suitable.

(1) Newton has a very active Community Service Unit, run by voluntary helpers. An organising committee of three persons, aged between nineteen and twenty-one, is meeting. This committee interviews persons willing to help. Three persons are due to be interviewed.

(2) The reading committee of the Drama Club has selected three one-act plays, one of which will be chosen as the club's entry for the annual drama festival. Each member of the committee outlines one of the plays. The members then make their choice.

(3) A person has been sold a faulty piece of equipment. He takes it back to the shop where it was purchased.

(4) The coach of the football/hockey/volleyball team has decided to drop a player from the team. This player has considerable ability but the coach, for reasons of his own, considers that the player should be rested. He asks the player to come to see him.

(5) Buses are off the road at weekends. Drivers refuse to take out the vehicles because there has been violence. A meeting has been called to

discuss what might be done. A representative from the bus company has agreed to attend the meeting. Also on the platform are the head teacher of the local comprehensive school, a police inspector and the local district councillor, who is in the chair. Members of the community make up the audience.

(6) Four persons have reached the final of a competition to find out the project which will be of most benefit to the community. Each competitor is given five minutes to outline his/her project and a further five minutes for questions by the three members of the judging panel. At the conclusion the panel announce the winner.

(7) The treasurer of a particular organisation prepares a balance sheet and presents it at a committee meeting.

(8) A youth organisation is looking for leaders. Two members of the organisation have been asked to visit a certain person to find out if he/she would be interested.

(9) A meeting of the members of a particular club has been called to consider what steps will be taken in view of the likely increase in rental of the club premises.

(10) Six senior pupils of a school have been called to the headmasters' study to meet a representative from the local hospital seeking help with the Christmas entertainment for patients.

(12) Four people are invited to the local radio broadcasting studio to take part in a weekly discussion programme.

(13) A member of a firm has been sent on a course. On her return she is called into the office to report to her employer.

(14) Members of a family discuss where they will go for their annual holiday.

Teaching points

All of the exercises will require to be expanded. Time must be allowed for preparation by those who are allocated roles. Tutors will be the best judges of exercises suitable for their own pupils.

iii CONVERSATION FOR LESS-ABLE PUPILS

What can be accomplished with less-able pupils will depend upon each particular class of pupils. It is important, however, not to underestimate the conversational potential of pupils or their capacity to engage in role-play. It is easy for a young teacher with no experience of working with pupils of limited intellectual ability to conclude that the spontaneous interaction required of role-players in a simulated situation is beyond them. This is not so—at least not any more than for pupils of intellectual potential.

During a role-play exercise with a group of honours graduates training for the teaching profession, the tutor turned to one student and tried to engage her in conversation without success. The student remained silent. After the role-play exercise was over, there was discussion regarding the usefulness of role-play in the classroom and one student said: 'Yes, I can see that role-play could be useful for some pupils, but with inarticulate ones it just wouldn't work.' The tutor replied, 'That might well be so, but wouldn't it depend upon what you mean by inarticulate pupils? We have just had a situation that defeated one of your own number, and in that instance the label inarticulate could have been pinned on her.'

A failure to respond in words may be due to reasons other than intellectual ones. To be found wanting in a situation where some verbal response is expected can be an embarrassment felt equally by the able and the less-able. The adjective 'inarticulate' may be appropriate to describe a pupil's performance in a particular situation but it would not necessarily be a valid comment on his or her conversational ability in general.

Conversation is a social habit as well as a means of self expression and if the habit is not well established, for whatever reason, self expression becomes more difficult. Thus it is not unknown for a person of considerable intellectual ability to have limited conversational skills.

Certainly the range of conversational topics is likely to be narrower for the less-able, and their working vocabulary is likely to be limited, but provided that role-play exercises are chosen for their relevance to the needs of pupils the desire to become involved is just as likely to be found in the less-able as it is in the able pupil.

Finally, although in this chapter it is assumed that the tutor will be a teacher operating in a classroom, there is no suggestion that the ideas about to be offered can be handled only by teachers. Were residential social workers in Children's Homes interested in the development of conversational ability among those for whom they had responsibility they too might find the following exercises and indeed many given in the previous chapter appropriate to their needs.

The main objectives of the exercises are to give pupils an opportunity to recognise and practise the behaviour that will be expected of them in everyday situations.

Suppose, then, that a tutor has taken over a class and is planning to use role-play to help her pupils develop their conversational skills, as a first stage, what might she do?

STAGE ONE

Sit down and listen to what the pupils are prepared to say. She should try to enjoy their conversations on their terms. If the tutor is a good listener, that is if the pupils get the impression that she is interested in them, that she really wants to hear what they have to say, and is finding the talk enjoyable, the chances are that they, the pupils, will become more relaxed. Confidence will then begin to build up. Once this happens the tutor can proceed to teach explicitly.

In Stage One what is important?

That pupils find the tutor to be a willing listener—someone with whom they can talk without fear of correction or judgement. That the pupils enjoy talking with each other and with the tutor. That the tutor enjoys the conversations.

What is unimportant?

Choice of words.
Speaking style of pupils.
Conversational topics.

What should tutors avoid?

Exerting pressure on any pupil to engage in conversation.
Commenting adversely on contributions or lack of them.
Taking over a conversation.

STAGE TWO: Getting Started

Less-able pupils are accustomed to failure, therefore exercises in this stage should be well within their capability so that the pupils may experience success. Praise is important. The following are suggested exercises.

First Exercise. Work in Pairs, A and B. A questions B. B replies. For instance:

A 'What's your name?'
B *replies*
A 'Where do you live?'
B *replies*
A 'Have you any brothers and sisters?'
B *replies*

Second Exercise

Repeat exercise with Bs asking the questions.

Third Exercise

As to think of three other questions to ask Bs.

Fourth Exercise

Bs to think of three different questions to ask As. Exercises can proceed simultaneously.

Fifth Exercise

Talking in front of others. Divide the class into two groups, approximately five in each group. The first group is in action, the second group listens. In turn each girl in the first group asks a question of another girl in her own group.

Sixth Exercise

Repeat exercise with second group in action and first group listening.
Note. If the fifth and sixth exercises are considered too difficult, in that pupils are being asked to talk in front of others, then of course, more practice in pairs is necessary first.

STAGE THREE: Chance Meeting

Role-play may now be introduced so that behaviour in situations outside the classroom can be practised.

First Exercise

Roles: two friends. Situation: The friends happen to meet in the street, they
 stop and chat, and then go their separate ways.

Second Exercise

Roles: two friends, and a third person known only to one of the friends.
Situation: The friends are sitting in a cafe chatting. The third person
 comes into the cafe, sees her friend and goes up to the table.
 Leave outcome to pupils.

Third Exercise

Roles: Three friends. Situation: Three friends are sitting chatting in a cafe.
   While this interaction is in progress the tutor should approach the group
and ask if she might join them. Leave outcome to pupils, with the tutor
responding to their lead.

Fourth Exercise

Roles: two neighbours, and a new neighbour. Situation: Two neighbours are
   talking and someone known to be a new neighbour passes by.
   After such exercises there may well be some discussion and pupils may
make suggestions for other chance meetings.

Points for discussion

   What it feels like to be left out of a conversation.
   How much easier it is to talk to friends than to strangers.
   Difficulties of talking with adults.
   Do some people find it easier to listen than to talk?
   Do some people never let anyone else get a word in edgeways?

STAGE FOUR: Listening

Ask pupils to list occasions when it would be important to listen to what
someone was saying to them. Role-play their suggestions. The following are
suggested exercises.

First Exercise

Roles: A is a stranger in town, B lives in the town. Situation: A is walking
   down the street when she is stopped by B who asks to be directed to X
   (perhaps the bus station, the post office, or B's own choice.)

Second Exercise

Roles: A is a pupil, B is a visitor to the school. Situation: B goes up to A in the
   playground and asks to be directed to the head teacher's room.

Third Exercise

Roles: Mother, Daughter. Situation: Mother is unable to leave the house and
   she asks her daughter to take a message to her neighbour.

Fourth Exercise

Roles: Mother, Babysitter. Situation: The babysitter arrives to let the mother go out. Mother gives the babysitter certain instructions.

Fifth Exercise

Roles: class teacher, pupil, parent. Situation: The class teacher gives the pupil a message to take to her parent. The pupil is to bring back the answer.
Note: this role-play would have three parts to it. The tutor might herself assume the role of class teacher if she felt this to be helpful. The tutor might also assume the role of the doctor in this following exercise.

Sixth Exercise

Roles: Doctor, Patient. Situation: The patient has been attending the clinic because she has had 'flu. This is her last visit. The doctor tells her how to look after herself during the next week or so.

STAGE FIVE: Telephoning

By this stage the pupils should be ready for more difficult tasks.
Place a table in a corner of the room and a chair beside it. Put a telephone on the table. Set up a second set of table, chair and telephone. The chairs should be so placed that when pupils sit in each they are back to back with each other, but able to hear the sounds of dialling. Give each pair the opportunity to dial a number, speak and answer. Once the procedure has become familiar the following exercises could be set.

First Exercise

Role: two friends. Situation: the friends have arranged to meet, but one of them now discovers that she cannot go out so she telephones her friend to explain.

Second Exercise

Roles: two friends, parent. Situation: One friend telephones her friend but the mother answers the telephone.

Third Exercise

Roles: mother, school secretary, Situation: The mother telephones the school and gives a message to the school secretary.

Repeat exercises as often as is desirable. Draw in observers to note the following points:

(1) Make sure number is correct before dialling.
(2) Speak so that the other person will hear easily.
(3) When answering—give name or telephone number.
(4) If required to deliver a message—be sure to get the exact one.

Fourth Exercise

Reinforce learning by playing a pre-recorded telephone conversation between persons unknown to pupils and during which certain deliberate mistakes are made. Ask pupils to listen and to spot deliberate mistakes.

Fifth Exercise

Seek the cooperation of the head teacher. Go over procedures for using a public telephone. Refer, perhaps, to a wall chart that contains all the necessary information. Give out the task, which is to give two pupils the necessary amount of money and then to send them out of school to a nearby telephone box where they will dial the school number. One will speak to two other pupils in turn, who will be waiting at the school telephone to receive the call. The exercise can be repeated with different pupils in action. The idea of sending out two pupils to each venue is that each might support the other.

Sixth Exercise

Introduce the telephone directory. Give pupils practice in looking up numbers. In class go over procedures and set role-play exercises to give practice in different types of telephone calls, for example:

(1) Telephone the exchange (*a*) to ask for a telephone number; (*b*) to report a fault in a neighbour's phone; (*c*) to send a telegram.
(2) Use the telephone to (*a*) call for an ambulance; (*b*) summon the Fire Brigade; (*c*) contact the police.

It is important that before proceeding to role-play the pupil playing the role of caller should know the message that has to be conveyed and those playing the other roles should also be familiar with what they have to say. For instance, should the caller dial 999 she should know what service she needs when she is asked for that information. Then when she is connected up with the service she must be ready to give the information. Similarly those who are playing the role of telephonist or, for example, police officer on telephone duty, need to respond precisely.

OTHER IDEAS

A.   Set up a series of role-plays to give pupils the opportunity:
  (1) to prepare for situations they may encounter in the process of looking for work;
  (2) to practise a future work role;
  (3) to gain information on the various situations and problems that affect the housewife;
  (4) to discuss problems of a more personal nature which they might be experiencing.

Note: In this connection the Question and Answer method of working outlined in the section dealing with Youth and Community Work might be appropriate and helpful.

B.   Use the tape-recorder.

Pupils may find tape-recording most enjoyable. They may well be surprised when they hear how good they really are. Such feelings are important for their progress in skills. Initially, however, some pupils may be scared of the microphone and the tutor should give plenty of time for anxieties to be overcome. Work will then be undertaken with enthusiasm.

C.   Ideas borrowed from the radio have the merit of familiarity but may be beyond the range of pupils at first. For a start, the roving reporter technique could be tried. Cast one pupil as the reporter. The reporter then conducts simulated street interviews to find out what pupils think about this or that product—this or that issue. When pupils have gained confidence in working with each other the tutor might seek the cooperation of school personnel so that interviews may be conducted with, for example, the head teacher or the school janitor. More ambitious still, pupils might visit and interview people beyond the school environment.

Finally, the tutor who is enthusiastic will devise role-plays that will encourage and stimulate learning among pupils. The tutor should find that this method of working appeals to pupils and gives them enjoyment and enhanced self-esteem.

PART TWO : SECTION THREE

SUBJECT TEACHING

Perhaps the main advantages to be gained from using role-play in the teaching of subjects in the curriculum are:
  (1) Role-play is different from other working methods.
  (2) Experience of role-play can be most enjoyable.
  (3) Participation gives pupils an opportunity to handle knowledge in dynamic circumstances.

  It would seem, however, that the technique of role-play is more suited to some subjects, for instance history, modern studies and languages, than to others, perhaps botany, physics, art or music.

  To illustrate the use of role-play for this purpose, a curriculum subject is chosen here which requires a different approach to role-play from what has been advocated in previous examples. The subject is Bible study

THE DIFFERENT APPROACH

Heretofore emphasis has been placed upon the need for adequate briefing, and the information suggested for briefing has related to imagined past events and situations which the role-takers could have experienced were the situation to be a real-life one. Further, in the subsequent interaction, it has been stressed that role-players should respond as each thinks fit with no interference from an outside source.

  If role-play is used to study events that have already happened, much of the information assembled in the briefing has basis in recorded fact. This inevitably confines interaction within certain limits and requires a different approach to role-play. Such a different approach must be adopted in Bible study, where pupils must be well briefed in the biblical events that did occur and the decisions that were taken by the various people involved in them. There is, however, some room for speculation. A pupil playing the role of innkeeper at Bethlehem could speculate upon the innkeeper's personality, and no doubt in the interaction would reveal imagined characteristics. That pupil, however, would require to curb his imagination on some factual matters and in his role-playing stay close to recorded history.

ROLE-PLAY IN BIBLE HISTORY

To illustrate the use of role-play in Bible study, certain events as recorded in the New Testament have been selected. These are:

(1) The Census as decreed by Caesar Augustus.

(2) The birth of a son to Mary and Joseph.

(3) Conflict induced by the teaching and preaching of Jesus of Nazareth.

(4) Crucifixion of Jesus of Nazareth.

The section is completed by listing encounters that might well have taken place and, therefore, would be plausible material for role-play.

The main objectives of this series of role-play exercises are to help pupils appreciate that the events of which they have some knowledge did actually happen, and that the people who lived through them were affected by them. There is no intention to use these exercises in order to preach the Christian Gospel. It is the historical figure of Jesus of Nazareth and his impact upon the lives of contemporaries that are being studied.

Should a tutor choose to use any of the suggestions, subsequent interaction might well give rise to discussion on purely religious matters, but that is not a declared objective of the exercises now to be outlined.

FIRST SET: The Census

Preparation. Recall historical facts, paying particular attention to the effects of the Roman Occupation. Go over geographical details. Refresh memories, perhaps through film strips, posters, etc., depicting life in Judea. Focus on Bethlehem. Lead up to the gathering of people in the town of Bethlehem for the Census decreed by Caesar Augustus.

Exercise A

Briefing. Ask pupils to record the kind of information they consider the people would be required to give. Ask pupils to list different categories of people likely to be in Bethlehem at the time of the Census. (Possible responses Merchants; tax-gatherers; civil servants engaged in the Census; shepherds; local residents; innkeeper and his family.) Ask each pupil to identify with one person on his or her own list. Try to achieve a range of personnel.

Ensure that two pupils take on the roles of civil servants. These two pupils will then: (*a*) set up tables for the Census taking; (*b*) agree on questions to be asked; (*c*) establish a procedure to be followed; (*d*) consider their own attitude as Romans to the citizens of Bethlehem, members of a conquered race.

The remainder of the pupils conduct their own personal briefing, giving themselves biographical information.

While this briefing is going on, the tutor should go round the class stimulating thought by asking such questions as:

(*a*) Is this the first Census you have ever conducted?

(*b*) So you are a merchant—what do you sell and where do you come from?

(*c*) What do you think of the influx of visitors into your own town?

(*d*) Have you found accommodation yet?

(*e*) You'll be expecting to do good business—is your inn fully booked up?

When the role-briefs are completed give out the situation brief.

Situation brief. This room has been taken over by the Roman authorities for the Census. These tables are the Census points. The two civil servants will explain how they wish the Census to be conducted and the procedures to be followed. (The civil servants might ask the people to line up in two columns; to approach one table when called and not before; to maintain complete silence throughout; etc.)

Interaction. When briefing is complete, the Census begins. It may be that, for instance, some Roman ruling is disobeyed and the authority of Rome is exercised as a consequence.

Before there is any discussion on the interaction, set another role-play.

Exercise B

Briefing. After the Census you congregate in small groups to talk over what happened. Did you resent being questioned by Rome? Were you disinterested? How inconvenient has it been for you to come to Bethlehem?

Interaction. The small group discussions, still in assumed roles.

Final Discussion. Ask each small group in turn to give a summary of what they talked about. Discussion may also centre around such issues as: use and misuse of power; rights of the 'common man'; indifference—complacency; collaboration with an occupying power; resistance and the consequences.

By the end of these two exercises the teacher hopes to find that pupils have greater understanding of the situation at that time in history as it might have affected ordinary people, among them Mary and Joseph.

SECOND SET: The Birth

Preparation. Recall the circumstances. Discuss the fact of the birth of Jesus from the point of view of different groups of people, for example: the innkeeper and his family, Herod and his Court, the people of Bethlehem, visitors to Bethlehem.

Exercise A

Situation brief. The Roman authorities have sent two investigators to Bethlehem to conduct a public inquiry to ascertain the truth of reports that have reached them of the birth of a male child. It has been decreed that certain people will be called upon to give evidence and be subjected to cross-examination. The enquiry will take place in public.

Briefing. Things to do. (*a*) Allocate roles, e.g. senior and junior investigators, persons summoned to give evidence, for instance—innkeeper, his wife, two natives of Bethlehem, two visitors, one from Nazareth and one from Jerusalem. (*b*) Each role-taker assembles his own information, which might include answers to such questions as: When did they hear of the Birth? Had they seen the baby? Had they seen Mary and Joseph coming into Bethlehem? Did they know Mary and Joseph? What was their attitude to the inquiry? (*c*) Establish procedural details such as: the order in which witnesses are called; the nature of questioning, e.g. led by senior and followed with cross-examination by junior.

Interaction. The public inquiry.

Possible Follow-up Exercise

Preparation: Recall the political position of Herod. Read Isaiah 40 and reflect upon the Prophecy from the Jewish and Roman viewpoints.

Situation brief. The two investigators are summoned to give their report to Herod. At the conclusion Herod issues instructions for the killing of male babies of two years and under.

Roles. Herod, his Chief of Staff, senior and junior investigators.

Interaction. The reporting and the consequent decision. (*Note.* This is a good example of the limit set upon interaction. Although it would be in order for, let us say, the Chief of Staff to try to persuade Herod not to come to the decision to slaughter the children, there is no avoiding the taking of the historical decision.)

Discussion. Such a role-play might well have much to say to today's pupils brought up in the era of reprisals, terrorism, sanctions and political unrest.

THIRD SET: Conflict

Preparation. Recall the beliefs of the Jewish people; the organisation of the Jewish Church; the relationship of the Jewish authority figures to the people; the political scene and the relationship between the Roman authority, the Jewish Church, the peoples of Judea and Galilee. Discuss and perhaps speculate upon the position of Jesus within the confines of his own family; points in the behaviour and teaching of Jesus that differed from what was expected of a Jew; ways in which the teaching of Jesus differed from the teaching of the Rabbis, or was considered to be politically subversive.

Exercise A

Situation. Jesus has left home to begin his work as a teacher and preacher.
Roles. Mary, Joseph, Mary Cleophas, two brothers.
Interaction. A family discussion. It is important to help pupils dismiss what knowledge they have of 'the future' and therefore of what is unknown to members of the family at this point in time. Jesus was in the family carpentry business so his going would have some effect upon the other men. Jesus as a member of a particular family had already shown behaviour that was difficult to understand, at least by some members of it.

Other Exercises

Situation. The fame of Jesus as a preacher is spreading. Different groups of people are beginning to be seriously affected.
Briefing. Ask pupils to sub-divide into one of the following groups—Pharisees; disciples; Roman Governor and staff; Zealots; other Jewish people.
Interaction. To set interaction off, read a passage from the Bible and then invite each group to hold a meeting to consider what action should be taken as a result of Jesus' behaviour. Suggested passages: Matthew 15. 1–9, the Pharisees are reproved; Matthew 21. 12–16, the casting out of merchants and money changers from the Temple; Luke 5. 27–31, eating and drinking with publicans; Luke 20. 19–26, obligations towards Caesar.

Meetings could proceed simultaneously if desired.

FOURTH SET: The Crucifixion

Preparation. Recall the events that lead up to the Crucifixion; the facts of the Crucifixion as revealed in the Bible.

Warm-up Exercise

Brief. Ask each pupil to identify with one person living in Jerusalem at the time of the Crucifixion and to consider it from that person's point of view.
Interaction. Invite each pupil in his or her assumed role to make some observation. If necessary the tutor should begin, with, for instance: 'I am Mary Cleophas. I came with my sister Mary who is the mother of Jesus and so I am his aunt. I didn't know how my sister would get through the day but somehow she did'; or, 'I am one of the Centurions detailed to carry out the Crucifixion. There are some jobs you like better than others, but you are in the Army and, well, that's that. You obey orders or else.'

Exercise A

Situation brief. Explain to the class that an Any Questions type of programme is being set up and people who were all closely identified with the Crucifixion have agreed to be present to answer any questions that may be put to them. Choose roles from those assumed in the Warm-up—for instance, Judas Iscariot; Mary Magdalene; Caiaphas; Simon Peter; Pontius Pilate. These persons are asked to sit out in front of the class.

Interaction. The questioning by the remainder of the class of the people on the part each played in the Crucifixion and their motives in doing so. Type of question envisaged—To Mary: What were your feelings towards Jesus? To Caiaphas: You were determined that Pontius Pilate would not hand Jesus over to you for judgment—why? To Pontius Pilate: In your cross-examination you could find no fault so how do you account for the decision you ultimately arrived at? To Simon Peter: Why did you say that you did not know Jesus?

Alternative Exercise

The format of this exercise is similar to that used in the television programme *Your Witness.* It is basically a debate during which people speak for or against a particular proposition. A chairman controls proceedings. There is a counsel for and a counsel against the proposition. Each counsel is given the same amount of time for the presentation of his or her own case. Each counsel may call as many witnesses as is necessary for establishing the case and each witness is called upon to give testimony and then be cross-examined by the opposing counsel. When the case opposing the proposition has been completed the case supporting it commences. Each counsel at the outset is given the same amount of time (say three minutes) to make an initial statement and at the conclusion a further allocation of equal time for summing up. The chairman then puts the proposition to the members of the general public, all of whom cast their vote for or against. The chairman keeps time and intervenes when time is running out.

Briefing. Select a question for debate, for example 'That the Crucifixion of Jesus of Nazareth was in the best interests of the Jewish people.'

Allocate roles: chairman, counsel and witnesses for the proposition, counsel and witnesses against the proposition, citizens.

Each individual citizen assembles his or her own information, which obviously includes an attitude towards the Crucifixion. Counsel engage in a briefing session with their own witnesses who also require to assemble their own information. The chairman explains the procedure to everyone, ensuring an understanding of such details as where each witness sits or stands while giving testimony, voting procedure, etc.

In particular the chairman emphasises the timing and informs counsel of the method to be adopted for warning them when time is running out.

The briefing for this exercise has to be thorough and will take a fair amount of time although not all pupils will be heavily committed. Each counsel and team of witnesses will need as much time as is necessary to prepare their case thoroughly. There is no point in beginning the interaction until all concerned are fully aware of their personal contributions and of the organisational details. *Your Witness* is a most interesting exercise for pupils who have the capacity to meet the demands of it. The tutor may play a role, possibly of chairman. The interaction may extend over a period of approximately one hour. A timetable might therefore be: Chairman's opening remarks, 4 minutes; counsel's opening statements, 3 minutes each; each case (including cross examination) 20 minutes; each summing-up, 5 minutes. Thereafter, voting.

FIFTH SET: Unrecorded Encounters

Ask pupils to speculate upon encounters that might have taken place between two or more persons. List suggestions. Possibilities:

(1) a meeting of the Pharisees when it became known that Jesus had entered Jerusalem;
(2) Simon Peter's meeting with other disciples after his denial of Jesus;
(3) meeting at which Zealots try to persuade Judas to betray Jesus;
(4) meeting between Judas and one person who knows that Judas is going to betray Jesus and who tries to persuade him not to do so;
(5) meeting between Mary of Magdala, Mary the mother of Jesus and some friends the night before the Crucifixion;
(6) meeting of the Pharisees after the trial;
(7) a family gathering during which one member returns home after being on duty at the Crucifixion;
(8) Pontius Pilate gives his report in person to the authorities in Rome;
(9) the return home of some person who witnessed the Crucifixion and who was a follower of Jesus;
(10) a meeting of Nazarenes after they have heard the news of the Crucifixion.

Select certain encounters, enough to involve all pupils in one exercise. Allocate roles. Leave groups to conduct their own briefing. Role-play each encounter in turn.

All such exercises are necessarily speculative, but if interaction remains within the bounds of plausibility it can provide pupils with interesting experiences. Perhaps, too, they may come to a better understanding of the human dilemma behind the historical events.

PART TWO: SECTION FOUR

SCHOOL TO WORK

A feature of school life today is the importance attached to vocational guidance. Teachers are appointed to posts that carry responsibility for counselling pupils on different aspects of the transition from school to work. In this section, a scheme of work that uses role-play as the main teaching medium is outlined.

THE SELECTION INTERVIEW

As the time to leave school approaches, pupils who know what they want to do and have the ability to undergo any training necessary to fulfil ambitions may well be outnumbered by those who either have no definite ideas concerning a future career or who have little hope of finding any employment.

It is safe to reckon, however, that nearly all pupils will be faced with at least one selection interview, at which each will hope to do well. As so much can hinge upon the outcome of an interview it is important that pupils should be adequately prepared for the experience. This set of exercises is designed to take pupils step by step through the process and has the following objectives:

(1) to establish the sequence of events that culminate in the appointment (or rejection) of an applicant for a particular post.
(2) to give pupils an opportunity to become familiar with the process.
(3) to let pupils experience something of what it may feel like to be interviewed.

The interviewing procedure is broken down into stages. Each stage is considered, first in theory and then through role-play.

The Stages: Advertisement
Application
Consequences of application
Preparation for interview
The selection interview
Decisions.

STAGE ONE: The Advertisement

Theory. At the outset it is advisable to define the term Interview and to contrast a selection interview with other types of interview, for instance interviews seen on television. Pupils should be asked to cut out from newspapers any advertisements for jobs that might interest them and to bring their cuttings to the class.

Using their examples consider:

(a) format of advertisements;
(b) information which advertisements contain;
(c) instructions that are given.

Discuss with pupils the thinking that precedes the drafting of an advertisement. For example the need of employers to:

(a) define the particular post so that the advertisement may carry accurate information for intending applicants;
(b) consider the type of person the firm wishes to recruit, in terms not only of qualifications but also of personal characteristics;
(c) determine wage/salary that will attract appropriately qualified applicants.

Role-play. Divide class into syndicates (7 or 8 persons in each).
Situation brief to each syndicate. Each syndicate represents a particular firm. A vacancy has occurred in one of the departments. A meeting is to be held to discuss the vacancy and to frame the advertisement. Those attending the meeting are: manager; departmental heads; personnel officer; secretary.

Before this meeting is held each syndicate will conduct its own briefing, and this will include: deciding the nature of the firm; allocating roles; determining in which department the vacancy has occurred and the nature of the post to be filled. When this briefing is completed the meeting may begin.
Discussion. Interaction will have produced advertisements. Discuss these with the pupils. Allow for re-drafting if necessary. Place all the advertisements on a noticeboard.

STAGE TWO: The Application

Theory. Consider letters of application—wording and lay-out. Discuss letter-writing and perhaps in particular:

(a) the importance employers attach to writing, spelling and composition when they are considering written applications;
(b) the need to include in the letter of application all requested information;
(c) the approach to referees for references (if required);
(d) the importance of weighing up an advertised post in the long term. For instance—Do hours of work appeal? Is the wage/salary offered sufficient? Promotion prospects? Personal interest in type of work.

Role-play. Prior to the role-play make copies of each advertisement, two copies per syndicate. Have a supply of stationery. Sub-divide each syndicate, thus doubling the number of operational units. Give to each unit a copy of one of the advertisements—not the one of their own devising in the previous role-play. (Two units will work on the same advertisement.)

Situation brief to units. Each unit contains members of the same family. One member wishes to apply for the advertised post. Assume that this person has the necessary experience/qualifications etc., to make application. Discuss the advertisement and consider what the letter of application should contain, then together as a unit compose it.

Before interaction each unit will require to determine family roles and which member is the applicant.

Discussion. When letters have been written—two per advertisement—go over various points with each unit. Give time for any amendments. Letters duly addressed should be collected for use in the next stage.

STAGE THREE: Consequences

Theory. When a letter of application has been despatched, one of several possible consequences will occur:

(a) the applicant will be offered the post without interview;
(b) the applicant will be called for interview;
(c) the applicant will be informed that the application has been rejected;
(d) the applicant will receive no communication.

The tutor should talk over the various consequences with pupils, helping them to appreciate the realities of job hunting and maybe the inevitable disappointments. The short leet system should be explained. The problem of holding out for a preferred job when offered a second-choice one should be discussed. The tutor should listen to the various points which pupils raise and to any reasons they may advance for their likely difficulties in securing employment.

It is not normal practice for firms to explain why an application has been rejected, yet there is always a reason why some applications are successful and others are not. Prejudices should be examined, also problems peculiar to particular categories of persons—for instance, the disabled.

The following role-play offers pupils the opportunity to look at the problem of selection from the point of view of employers.

Role-play. Units re-unite in syndicates and revert to firms as they were in Stage One. Each firm is given the two letters of application in answer to the vacant post which they advertised.

Situation brief to firms. Assume again the same roles within the firm. You have two letters of application before you. Consider each carefully. One applicant has to be called for interview while the other is held in reserve. Come to your decisions.

Discussion. Each firm is asked to announce its decision and to give reasons why one applicant was preferred to the other.

STAGE FOUR: Preparation for Interview

Theory. Consider the expectations that employers may have of persons they will be interviewing and therefore matters applicants should take account of in their preparation. List expectations, e.g. that applicants:

    should be neat and tidy in appearance;

    should have given some thought to being questioned;

    should be able to answer questions put to them;

    should be able to express thoughts clearly;

    should appear to be interested in the post for which they have applied.

  List what might be done in preparation. Applicants might:

    consider the kind of questions that may be asked of them.

    organise their own thoughts regarding the post, and their reasons for applying.

    have ready any certificates, etc. that should be taken to the interview.

    on the day of interview attend to personal grooming and leave home with time to spare in order to ensure punctuality.

Discuss with pupils the difficulties they consider they might experience at the interview. No doubt the problem of overcoming nervousness will loom large. Try to help pupils appreciate that the majority of employers, well aware that young applicants will be nervous, will consequently make allowances. Equally, stress that the tongue-tied or the head-hanging applicant may be 'working himself or herself out of a job' despite capability. Employers are not mind-readers and it is up to applicants to demonstrate suitability. To emphasise and to give practice in the answering of questions set the following exercise:

First Role-play. Divide the class into buzz groups, three pupils in each.

Situation Brief. In each group there is an interviewer and one person who has agreed to be interviewed on a subject of that person's own choice. One person will watch. Agree on roles. Let the interviewee declare the subject. Then each buzz group begins interaction.

Second and third Role-plays follow, changing roles to allow each pupil to be questioned. The interviewers in the second or third role-play may introduce degrees of difficulty to make the experience more testing, for instance, increasing the rate at which questions are put; querying answers; or by putting questions in an abrupt manner.

Discussion. This will be centred around experiences in the buzz groups.

Points that may have emerged.

  (1) Feeling nervous affects behaviour.

  (2) If one is hurried into replying one tends to say something one does not mean.

(3) An interviewee may be put off his stride merely by the way the interviewer looks at him.

(4) If one doesn't know the answer to a question one can feel a fool.

(5) It can be difficult to find words.

Discuss the various points that pupils raise. They may be helped by further practice in the giving and answering of questions.

STAGE FIVE: The Selection Interview

Recall points discussed in Stage Four. Consider different ways in which employers conduct their interviews. For example:

    (*a*) procedures for reception of applicants;

    (*b*) lay-out of furniture and seating;

    (*c*) interviewing techniques from informal to formal;

    (*d*) use of two or more interviewers.

If a suitable film is available it should be a useful learning agent.

First Role-play. Pupils work in syndicates used in Stages 1 and 3.

Briefing to syndicates. Each syndicate is a firm. In each syndicate there is one person who has made successful application for a vacant post in another syndicate's firm. That person will be interviewed. The remaining people in the syndicate all played a specific role in Stage One as either manager, head of department, personnel officer or secretary. One of these will be the interviewer. Each syndicate will select the interviewer and set up a corner of the room as an interview room—placing the chairs, etc. While the applicants are preparing themselves to be interviewed members of the firm should consider the kind of information that is needed and therefore some questions that the interviewer will put.

When the briefing is completed the applicant is called into the interview room and the interview proceeds. Observers are suitably placed so that they do not interfere in the interaction. It is not a panel interview.

Interaction—the selection interviews.

Discussion. Within each syndicate pupils should go over their own experiences and consider certain questions, for instance:

    Should the applicant have got the job? If yes, why. If no, why not?

    Did applicants consider that they did themselves justice?

    What view did the interviewers have of the applicant's behaviour?

Pupils should try to be as honest with each other as possible so that each may learn something of value for the future.

Second Role-play. Class still operating in syndicates and independently but for this exercise a degree of difficulty is introduced.

Brief to syndicates. Another applicant is to be interviewed for the same job. One of the observers in each syndicate should take on the role of applicant and another that of interviewer. While the new applicants are briefing themselves the new interviewers come for their briefing.

Brief to interviewers. Introduce a degree of difficulty. Suggestions:

Leave applicant standing while you continue to read papers.

Be formal in your approach to applicant.

Put questions in a brisk, matter-of-fact manner.

Decide what you will do but don't behave in an extreme fashion.

Brief to syndicates. Not all interviews proceed in the same way. Not all interviewers have time to put applicants at ease. Different things happen. In the following role-play the employers have been asked to introduce a degree of difficulty into the interview. If the applicant is made to feel nervous, that's good because at a real interview the applicant may well be nervous and still want to do his or her best.

Interaction—the interview.

Discussion. General discussion with pupils saying what happened at their own interviews.

Third Role-play. Plenary session. Select a different type of appointment, perhaps something in the nature of the following:

For some years now a national society has been organising a Holiday Abroad scheme for school pupils to promote better understanding among young people in Europe. This year the holiday is to Denmark and this year also the pupils' school has been offered two places. Five pupils have applied and each will be interviewed by three members of a panel.

Steps to be taken

(1) Tutor outlines situation to pupils.

(2) Additional information regarding the society and the scheme are agreed.

(3) Roles are determined.

(4) The three panel members will conduct their own briefing and determine and declare to others what their exact role is to be, e.g. head teacher, representative from the organising society, representative from the Parent/Teacher Association.

(5) Applicants will consider their position, independently of course.

(6) With the above aspects of briefing completed, an interview room should be set up, the order in which applicants will be interviewed must be agreed, and all other preparations made.

Interaction. With thorough briefing and pupils ready for such a role-play, the interaction is likely to proceed at a significant level and be enjoyed by panel members, applicants and observers.

Discussion. This might be conducted in three groups:
(a) Panel to determine whom they will select and why.
(b) Applicants to discuss their own experiences.
(c) Observers to reflect on the interaction and perhaps come to their own choice of applicants.

In general discussion the tutor may help pupils to summarise for themselves the different learning points.

STAGE SIX: The Decision

Discuss with pupils the problem of selection and rejection. From their own experience, perhaps of sport, this will be a familiar area.

Perhaps consider with pupils the role of teacher, contrasting it with that of a future employer. What responsibility has an employer towards those who seek employment in his or her firm? To what extent can applicants expect employers to make allowances for them in an interview situation?

Each tutor will know the issues that his or her own pupils will want to discuss. School leavers should have opportunity to voice their hopes and fears to an involved, understanding adult.

Whether or not it will be helpful to reinforce theory through role-play will depend on circumstances: if this is felt to be desirable, the following exercise may be tried:

Role-play. After discussion on the problems of selection and therefore rejection, and using Stage Five exercise, ask the panel to call back successful candidates to the interview room in order to apprise them of the decision and to give them an opportunity to ask questions.

A Second Role-play. One of the panel members speaks to unsuccessful candidates.

Discussion. No doubt in the discussion the feelings both of those who give decisions and of those who receive them will be considered.

Summary. This scheme of work has been designed to help pupils become more familiar with the procedures surrounding selection interviews. As a consequence of participation pupils should:
(a) have had opportunity to express their own anxieties;
(b) have had opportunity to practise interviewing and being interviewed;
(c) feel much better prepared to cope with future interviews than they were at the outset.

PART TWO: SECTION FIVE

YOUTH AND COMMUNITY

In this section the writer has in mind readers who are concerned particularly with the training of people in the broad field of youth and community work. It is hoped that the ideas advanced in this section will be useful not only for tutors involved in the training of professional workers but also for the many who are attached to youth and/or community organisations of one kind or another as training officers. That being so it should be recognised that when the words 'student' and 'youth and community worker' are used they refer respectively to people undergoing training and to workers in the field.

Equally with teachers, youth and community workers require to develop observational and conversational skills to a high degree. It is therefore important to appreciate that comments and exercises in these areas which were offered in Sections One and Two, are considered to be as relevant and valuable in the context of youth and community work as in that of teaching.

Six different ways in which role-play may be organised are introduced. Each method of working has been labelled, for convenience, and will be described. Views will be expressed on the suitability of the different methods in relation to training groups.

METHODS

Questions and Answers
Consequences
Diversions
Check List
In-Tray
Doubling.

The section is concluded with accounts of how role-play was used to promote social skills firstly in a youth club and secondly in a Scottish List D School for girls.

QUESTIONS AND ANSWERS

This title has been given to a method that is concerned essentially with the posing and answering of questions. It is a simple device and suitable for use by adults in their regular work with small groups of adolescents where their main objective is to encourage people to express their own views and discuss their

141

own difficulties. It is assumed that at a training session for students the method is being introduced to them as one that they should find useful in certain future work situations. The hope is that as a consequence of participation students will:

(a)   reflect upon the need of young people—particularly those in residential situations—to discuss matters that concern them with interested adults;

(b)   evaluate the method as a means by which conversation may be encouraged.

Steps to take:

(1)   Prior to the training session, cut out a selection of readers' letters from magazines—ones that are acceptable to the student group.

(2)   At the training session divide the group into units of five to six persons, and ask one person to be the leader.

(3)   Brief the units along the following lines.
'As you know, magazines of all kinds receive letters from their readers seeking information and/or advice. Presumably all letters are considered and some are selected for reply in print. You are asked to accept that those of you who have agreed to be leaders are, in fact, sub-editors of the section of the magazine that is handling the letters and that the others in each unit are all members of the sub-editorial team.'

(4)   Give one letter to each sub-editor, with the following instructions:
'Sub-editors are asked to read out their given letter to their team; to discuss its contents; and to compose the reply. The reply which the magazine has given is folded over: sub-editors should not reveal the reply until their own reply has been agreed.'

(5)   Interaction. Discussion of letters within each team and composition of replies.

(6)   Reading of magazine replies by each sub-editor, and discussion.

(7)   A second round of letters may be handed out and treated similarly.

(8)   Discussion. This would include not only evaluation of the method but also of the social need to be met.

Teaching points

(1)   This method of working may have no appeal for the particular tutorial group: if so, it should not be pursued.

(2)   An examination of women's magazines reveals that letters cover a wide range of problems and not exclusively deeply personal ones. Response to the method might well hinge upon choice of first letters. It is probably wise therefore to select ones that seek specific information before introducing any that ask for advice on personal problems.

(3)   The idea of hiding the magazine's reply until the groups' replies have been agreed is interesting in that members of the group are keen to

know what that reply was and to contrast it with their own. (Incidentally, magazine replies can provide participants with useful information.)

(4) A valuable feature of the method, and one that is particularly important in working with adolescents, is that it allows participants to discuss a problem that some other person has presented and in so doing perhaps to find that the discussion is helpful for an undeclared problem of their own. To that extent, therefore, participants are given a legitimate 'mask' which can be kept on for as long as need be. Ultimately, each worker will hope that through role-play there will be created the kind of atmosphere in which the young people feel no need to operate from behind a front, and in which they can then begin to talk openly about matters that concern them.

(5) The increase in the number of radio and television programmes that are devoted to the posing and answering of questions suggests that there is a social need to be met. It is fruitful to speculate on the reasons why people write to a magazine or phone-in to a radio or television programme in preference to contacting a more readily available person. With regard to young people, could one of the reasons be that readily available adults are not always prepared to take time to listen to problems brought to them?

(6) Particularly in a residential situation, the worker has a responsibility to provide an opportunity for young people to discuss matters that concern them. It is not always easy to find time for discussion or to persuade young people, singly or collectively, to engage in conversation. Nevertheless, this is a very important aspect of working with young people. Workers should do whatever they can to encourage discussion.

The following variations are offered as further vehicles for stimulating discussion.

VARIATIONS FOR USE WITH ADOLESCENTS

(1) After the original role-play, suggest that before the next meeting of the group each person write a letter to a particular type of magazine. (This to be agreed) These letters will be placed in a box and at the next meeting the editorial team will discuss and answer letters in turn in the manner of the first role-play.

Note. It may be advisable to suggest that letter writers use *nom-de-plumes* so that during the editorial conference no one will know the authors and all will be able to discuss their own problems as well as those of others.

(2) When the editorial device begins to pall, switch to a panel of experts—prior to the meeting, certain members are asked to write a

letter on a matter of concern. In turn, at the group meeting, each writer reads out his or her own letter and members of the panel voice their opinions.

(3)   Prior to the meeting give certain people a poem, or the lyric of a song, which they are presumed to have written (or allow them their own choice of poem, etc.) At the meeting members in turn read out their poem and are asked questions about it by the others.
How did the poem come to be written and why?

(4)   If exercise 2 and 3 have been undertaken the masks are likely to be off and if that has happened then it may be possible to engage in a question and answer exercise that looks at problems from different points of view. Select an article from a newspaper, for instance: 'An elderly woman who lived alone died when fire broke out in her home yesterday.' Cast members of the group in specific roles: neighbour, fireman, police constable, relative, nurse, social worker. Each person in his or her own role replies to questions posed by the tutor.
Alternatively, two or three members are the questioners.

Ideas beget ideas. Start on one exercise, then developments and variations follow. It is possible that from such beginnings there could emerge an advisory service for adolescents, perhaps manned by adolescents. That this would be in the long term is recognised, but such a service within a community is well worth encouraging.

CONSEQUENCES

This is a convenient label for a method of working which starts with the given situation and then develops into other situations suggested by the interaction that occurs. It is suitable for students at any stage in training, with the proviso that they have become familiar with the technique of role-play. The objective is to inject a greater degree of realism into role-play by focusing on the consequences of action taken by individuals. An initial role-play exercise is set. It is played through, but instead of discussion the tutor sets a second role-play and then another so that students engage in a series of situations all stemming from an initial one. This follows the pattern in life. A attends a meeting and as a consequence of a decision taken is involved in other conversations, meetings and problems. Perhaps the easiest way of describing the organisation is to give an account of work that was done with a particular student group.

Example. This initial situation was described by a student. It happened when she was on placement:

One evening at the Club a known trouble-maker handed in his jacket. He laid it on the table at the door where members were encouraged to place valuables, coats, etc., for safe-keeping. I was on duty and I picked up the jacket. As I was hanging it up a knife fell out of the pocket. Offensive weapons were not permitted in the club so I decided to go straight to the Leader's office to report the incident. I called for someone to take over my duty.

First Role-play. Roles. Club leader, and student on placement (played by the student).

Briefing. The student who outlined the situation supplied extra information. Interaction took place during which the Leader agreed to see the member in question. At the end of this role-play and before any discussion took place, the tutor intervened, saying to the leader: 'Let us assume that you have sent for Bob Green. Decide how you are going to approach this interview'. The tutor told another student to play the role of Bob Green.

Second Role-play. This was not a re-cap of the interaction that did occur in the real situation. Encounter between the Leader and Bob Green.

The Leader played this coolly. He placed the weapon on his desk before Bob came into the office and began to busy himself with paperwork. When Bob came in he left him standing for quite some time and then looked up and said, 'Pick up your knife'. Bob was 'thrown' but he picked up his knife and waited. 'Now go', said the Leader and returned to his papers. Bob went.

The effect on observers was considerable but before any discussion on the effectiveness or otherwise of the Leader's behaviour towards Bob could take place the tutor immediately set the group another exercise:

The story gets around that the Leader took no action whatever and the student was very annoyed. She felt that she had been let down and her authority undermined. Other members of staff sympathised with her and indeed some were very critical of the Leader's handling of the situation. Two of them decide to see the Leader. Two volunteers?

Third Role-play. Roles: Leader, and two members of staff.

This encounter was not productive. Both members of staff felt that the Leader's action had weakened the position of all members of staff and particularly in their relations with difficult members. The Leader defended his action and the meeting concluded with marked deterioration in relationships.

TUTOR: At the next meeting of the management committee a member, whose two children attend the youth club regularly, asked the chairman if the Leader might give some explanation of an incident which incurred in the club. He had received rather disturbing accounts of how a boy brought a knife into the club, was reported to the Leader who took no action.

Fourth Role-play. Roles: Chairman, leader, member who will ask the question, and other members. Discussion followed the conclusion of the fourth role-play.

Teaching points

It should be noted that the tutor did not plan the series of exercises before-hand but, from the interaction that did occur, set the next exercise and what happened in that one led to the third and ultimately the fourth.

The student cast initially in the role of Leader played this role throughout the series of exercises. This is essential if students are to experience the consequences of decisions. It is all too easy in a role-play to ignore probable consequences, but by requiring students to face up to consequences role-play moves nearer real-life experience. Equally this method of working focuses on accountability: people are affected by decisions that others take. Advanced students should be brought to sharp awareness of this fact.

DIVERSIONS

This has an objective similar to that of Consequences: it attempts to make interaction more life-like. Also it is more suited to advance students than to those in the early stages of their training.

Description. A professionally produced training film is concerned with the work of the school counsellor. In one scene the counsellor is in the course of an important interview with one pupil when a second pupil creates a diversion by rushing unheralded into his office in an obviously distressed state. Normally a role-play would be concerned with a counsellor/pupil inter-view but this method of working through the planned diversion adds an extra dimension to the interaction.

Procedure. Set a role-play. Without informing interactants that anything unusual is going to happen pre-arrange the desired diversion. For example:

(*a*)   entry of a colleague requesting or giving information;
(*b*)   entry of a canteen worker with a cup of tea;
(*c*)   entry of someone with a note, the contents of which demand urgent attention;
(*d*)   telephone rings and the caller is difficult to interrupt.

VARIATIONS

(A) Set a role-play. During the briefing give the worker information/instruc-tion. For example:

(*a*)   You have someone else coming to see you. Her appointment is in five minutes.
(*b*)   At some point you must explain to the person that you will be handing over the problem to a colleague as you are going off on holiday.

(B) Set a role-play. During briefing give the person who has the problem some instruction that has to be followed. For example:

(*a*)   At some point you must ask for a second opinion.

(*b*)   At some point you must ask if you could make a 'phone call as you promised to be home by 4.00 p.m. and it is now almost 4.00 p.m.

Teaching points

Diversions should be plausible in the context of the roles and the simulated situation.

Only the person(s) due to create the diversion have prior knowledge of it.

Diversions may be of considerable importance and significance as was the case in the scene from the film but could be apparently trivial like the ringing of the telephone, or the cup of tea.

If, for example, the diversion calls for the worker to leave the office, the role-play should be continued to allow for the return of the worker to the office. It would be possible to play the return in two ways: (*a*) the visitor is still in the office; (*b*) in the interval, the visitor has left so what action might the worker take?

Experience has shown that this way of working is exceedingly valuable and principally for the discussion on options that Diversions promote.

CHECK LIST

The Check List method of working is concerned essentially with the development of skills. It requires participants to identify tasks, to consider their own likely performance, and to participate in exercises designed to improve their performance. The method is suitable for students who have had some field-work experience. The aim is to offer students an opportunity to:

(*a*)   identify skills necessary in their own present or future youth and community work;

(*b*)   consider their own present level of competence;

(*c*)   recognise their efficiency gap;

(*d*)   organise their own behaviour and reduce the gap by means of developing skills.

STEP ONE. Ask students to:

(*a*) list a range of persons with whom the worker comes into contact in the course of his/her duties, e.g. club members, senior citizens, disabled persons, voluntary helpers, various professional workers, local authority personnel, etc.;

(*b*) list settings in which encounters occur, e.g. club rooms, church halls, private homes, offices, residential homes, etc.;

(*c*) list functions that workers perform, e.g. to advise, to instruct, to organise, to inform, to persuade.

STEP TWO

Ask students using their own Check List as reference, to select *one task* which, if now called upon to undertake, they would feel able to perform efficiently, and *ONE OTHER TASK* which might present difficulty. For example:

Student A would feel competent to instruct a group of beginners in orienteering;
would find it difficult to present a report at a meeting.

Student B would feel competent to give a talk provided that he knew his subject;
would find it very difficult to persuade a group to take a particular course of action.

Student C would feel reasonably sure of herself giving out information, no matter what the circumstances were;
would find it difficult to handle a disciplinary matter.

Student D feels reasonably comfortable when working with small groups but has great difficulty in facing a large group, particularly if the group consists of persons a lot older than himself.

STEP THREE

In consultation with students devise a programme of work.

STEP FOUR

Role-play. Give each student a task consistent with his or her own specifications of the easy task. Each then in turn has an opportunity to undertake the task.

STEP FIVE

Evaluation. This comes after the completion of the given task. Here is the time for re-appraisal. Students should be encouraged to be self-critical. How the evaluation is conducted is a matter for each individual tutor. It is quite a good idea, however, to give students a list of questions for written replies. For example:

(a)   Was preparation for the task sufficient?
(b)   In what way might preparation have been more thorough?
(c)   Did you know what you were trying to do?
(d)   Were the group and the objectives you set realistic, particularly in relation to the time at your disposal?
(e)   To what, specifically did you attribute your nerves at the beginning of your task?
(f)   Did you use time to the best advantage?
(g)   Was your work pitched at the appropriate level?
(h)   What attempt did you make to check that the information you gave out was understood?
(i)   Did you make sufficient allowance for difficulties?
(j)   What effort did you make to understand the point of view of the others?

Of course, the nature of the given tasks determine the questions that should be posed.

STEP SIX

Students in turn perform a more difficult task, again one based on their own specifications. Possible tasks, based on the sample responses quoted in Step 2, are now listed, two per student:

Student A

(1)   You are required to take the first of a course of ten lessons on orienteering for beginners.
(2)   You have been asked to attend a conference and are now required to report at the next meeting of the group responsible for your attendance.

Student B

(1)   Give a talk on a subject of your own choice to an adult group of around twenty people. Maximun time is ten minutes.
(2)   You have been trying to organise a scheme of voluntary help. Choose your own scheme. You are looking for volunteers. The headteacher of the local school has agreed to allow you to speak to the sixth-form pupils.

6

Student C

(1) You have been investigating the possibility of taking a group abroad. You have acquired the necessary information and now meet members who have expressed interests.
(2) You are in charge of a particular group of persons. The behaviour of some members has been unsatisfactory in certain respects. You decide to speak to the group as a whole.

Student D

(1) You have a certain project in mind. You ask for an interview with the person who has power to grant you permission to undertake the project.
(2) You have a certain project in mind. You require permission from a particular committee. You are invited to state your case before this committee, some members of which hold influential positions in the community.

Teaching points

Students should be given advance notice of tasks.
Students should set up their own role-plays.

IN-TRAY

The In-Tray method assumes that a specific position is held by a particular person and to that person comes various letters, 'phone calls, problems, reports, etc., that call for decisions. The object is to promote good decision-making. This way of working is considered to be suitable for students at an advance stage of training.

Prior to the setting up of In-Tray exercises the tutor should be concerned to help students appreciate the different stages of the decision-making process, so that the role-plays give students an opportunity to apply theoretical knowledge in the simulated situations.

STEP ONE

In consultation with students:

(a) Determine position and setting. For present purposes this is taken to be Manager of a community centre.
(b) Create a specific community centre and this will involve details such as: name, accommodation, facilities, membership, staff, opening hours.

(c)   Place this centre in a specific community: name, geographical position,
      population, employment, schools, housing, facilities for recreation, etc.
         It is advisable to create a Centre, set it in a community and presume
      that it is in this Centre that the manager works. This cuts down briefing
      during the progress of In-Tray exercises and does encourage realism.
      Additional information may be supplied as different role-plays demand.
(d)   Display information regarding the Centre and the community so that it
      can be referred to easily.

STEP TWO

Prepare the manager's role brief. This should include certain basic information such as: qualifications, previous experience, year of appointment,
record since appointment, relations with staff, other professional workers, etc.
Note. It is advisable to presume that the manager is competent, has reasonably
good relations with his staff, and is well regarded in the community. This encourages students to try to play the role competently. All who take on the role
of manager also take on these basic characteristics.

STEP THREE

Prepare In-Tray material. It is probably advisable for the tutor to undertake
this task, at least for the first round of exercises. Thereafter the tutor may
choose to ask students from their own experience to suggest material.

INTRODUCTION

(1)   Describe the In-Tray method of working.
(2)   Outline educational objective.
(3)   Recall the decision-making process.
(4)   Go over the three briefs with students, i.e. manager, centre and
      community.
(5)   Select three students each of whom will in turn play the role of manager
      at the next training session.
(6)   Explain that each manager will be required to take a task from the In-
      Tray, do his or her own preparation, and at the next meeting perform
      that task.
(7)   Invite the three students to take one task each from the In-Tray
      material.

6*

Exercises

(1) If necessary recall information contained within briefs.
(2) The first students sets up his or her own exercise and proceeds with the role-play.
(3) The second student.
(4) The third student.

Note. The number of students undertaking tasks will depend on available time and on the nature of the In-Tray material. It is advisable to set a time limit on individual role-plays to ensure that the full programme for each session is completed. On occasions students should be given material one session before they are required to take action. In life, however, decisions have often to be taken immediately on receipt of a letter or message and sometimes a person appears in an office unheralded and with a problem of which a manager has had no advance warning. Time given to students for preparation should therefore be realistic.

Teaching points

Each role-play will bring its own material for discussion. It is important that tutor and students consider behaviour during interaction and reflect upon the decision-making technique of each manager. No doubt the tutor will be asking questions and among these might well be:

(1) Did the manager look at the problem from all angles before taking a decision?
(2) Did the manager have enough information upon which to base a decision?
(3) Was any attempt made to check on given information?
(4) Was the problem identified?
(5) Was there agreement on the nature of the problem?
(6) Were the long-term as well as the short-term consequences considered before the decision was taken?
(7) Was the manager competent to deal with that specific problem?
(8) To what extent did the raised feelings affect the decision-making process?
(9) The manager took an unpopular line: what might be some of the consequences of such a decision?
(10) What steps were taken to ensure that the persons affected by the manager's decision were made aware of it?
(11) What was the most that the manager could have accomplished at this meeting?

(12) Would the people presenting the problem to the manager be confident that their interests were being safe-guarded?

(13) The manager had advance notice of the problem: was there sufficient preparation prior to the interview?

(14) Were all persons involved in the situation consulted prior to decision?

(15) Did the manager have any authority to take that decision?

(16) What methods were used to implement the decision?

SUGGESTIONS FOR IN-TRAY MATERIAL

(1) Anne and Sheila are friends, both aged sixteen. Both have been attending the centre regularly for several years. At a recent meeting of the centre management committee, Sheila was made a leader of a small group of girls in the ten to twelve age range. She has always been very keen to help with the younger girls and has made a very good start with her group. An interesting programme has been planned. Anne has been hurt by Sheila's promotion. She considers that she should have been given a group as well. Unlike Sheila, however, Anne has never really shown any interest in working with younger members. She asked if she could see the manager and said what it was about. The manager agreed to see her the following day.

(2) Mary Green is a very good badminton player. Some months ago she put in a request to the management committee that she be given permission to start a junior section of the Badminton Club. After discussion it was agreed that it might be possible to accommodate the juniors in the hall on Mondays between 6.30 and 8.00 p.m., if the Country Dance Group were prepared to use the lesser hall until 8.00 p.m. This the group agreed to do. Miss Green was given permission then to start the junior section. All went well at first. Numbers increased from twelve to around eighteen and the juniors enjoyed their sessions as Mary was a very good coach. Gradually however, numbers dwindled. There were Mondays when Mary didn't turn up and on other occasions she arrived quite late. The Country Dance Group were dissatisfied and asked to see the manager. The manager was aware of the arrangements that had been made and of the subsequent problems regarding Mary's attendance and the decrease in membership.

(3) Letter from a parent to manager.

Dear Ms Y,

I write to complain about an incident that happened in the centre on Friday night. My son, Jim, and his three friends were playing table tennis when another group of older boys came into the room expecting to have a game. As the table was occupied, one of the boys grabbed the table tennis ball while the others tried to take the bats from Jim and his friends. There was a scuffle and the noise attracted people including one of your assistants. This person came into the room and without waiting to hear anyone's story turned off the lights. He switched them on again and told everyone to clear out, or he would call the manager. My son was not responsible for the disturbance and I strongly object to the way in which he was treated. I trust that you will give this matter your attention. I may add that this is not the first time your assistant has acted unfairly.

Yours, etc.

(4)   The nightly report book written up by the senior member of staff on duty records that an incident occurred between canteen staff and certain members. The report states that several members failed to return dishes to the coffee bar and as business was brisk and the canteen staff were at full stretch this proved to be an irritation. Members were repeatedly asked to return dishes, but they did not do so. Tempers flared. Mrs Blue refused to serve and closed the coffee bar.

(5)   A member of the centre is a painter to trade and is helping with the decoration of the coffee bar in his free time. A group of four are working with him. The manager notices that the painter is using materials not ordered by the centre and asks the painter if he has 'acquired' these from his firm. This is readily admitted.

(6)   Letter from a part-time worker to manager.

Dear Jim,

I am sorry that I must resign from my work in the centre. As you know I have been associated with the Junior Club for ten years but I feel I can no longer continue with the work. This decision has not been taken lightly. I would like to thank you, for the consideration which you, in particular, have always shown to me.

Yours, etc.

(7)   Note from caretaker.

For the past three Wednesdays I have had to clear away equipment in the sports hall. This is not my job. I spoke to the leader about this last week but there was no improvement this week. Would you please deal with this.

John

(8)   Note from manager's secretary.

Mr Light phoned to say that he would be unable to take his discussion group tonight and would you please stand in for him?

(9)   Letters received from applicants for the post of assistant handyman.

(*a*) Dear Sir,
I shall be able to come for interview at 2.00 p.m. on Monday.
Yours truly
M. White

(*b*) Dear Sir,
I got your letter asking me to come for interview on Monday at
2.30 p.m.
This will be alright.
Y. Black

Diary entry: MONDAY—Interviews—2.00—2.30p.m.
                              2.30—3.00 p.m.

(10) The manager receives a phone call from the head teacher of the local
primary school regarding possible use of the centre premises by the
school for a specific period. The manager agrees to call at the school to
see the head teacher.

(11) There has been considerable dissatisfaction among the canteen
personnel. One member of staff appears to be the source of discontent.
The manager is aware of that person's increasing unpopularity and of
the effect that this is having upon the others. The manager asks this
person to come to the office.

(12) Two weeks ago a student arrived at the centre on placement. Already it
is apparent that the student is not settling down. The manager talks to
the student.

Finally, a set of unprepared encounters—so the manager in each role-
play has no advance warning. The student in the pair-role in each
situation requires advance notice so that he/she may assemble his/her
own information.

(1) Into the office one morning comes a police sergeant.
(2) The door of the office opens and a member tells the manager that she
has just had her purse stolen.
(3) The phone rings—could the manager please get a message to Mrs
Brown in the canteen? There has been a slight accident and she is
needed at home.
(4) A parent arrives. Her daughter is in trouble with the police. Would the
manager help?

(5)   A sales representative arrives hoping to interest the manager in equipment.

(6)   A survey is being conducted in the area to ascertain in what particular ways the different organisations/centres might assist with the project of teaching English to immigrant adults. An interviewer calls to see the manager.

DOUBLING

This can have considerable appeal despite the fact that the style bears no relation to what obtains in real life.

Two persons are cast in each role in a simulated situation. They are called A1 and A2, B1 and B2, and so on according to the number of roles to be played. A1 assumes the role and interacts with B1, C1 etc. Meantime A2, B2 and C2 each sit near to their own No. 1. The function of the No. 2s is to identify with the statements of their No. 1 and to listen to the statements of the other No. 1s. Then if, for example, A2 considers that A1 is not operating as effectively as is necessary she taps A1 on the shoulder and immediately the two change places. There is little or no interruption in the interaction as all the other No. 1s relate to A2 as if there has been no change in personnel. Similarly other 2s will wish to change places with their own No. 1 and at some later point further interchanges will occur.

The one who sits nearby, i.e. the *alter ego*, may operate only by tapping and changing places. In other words A2 does not make the balls for A1 to fire. On the contrary there is no communication between A1 and A2. The one in the silent chair listens to what is being said and if his 'double' is losing the point or getting the worst of an argument, by tapping he can take over the talking position and participate in the interaction. The person in the talking position must give way when he receives the signal but can, of course, come back into action by the same method.

Suitability. This is a useful device for students at the beginning of a training course when, perhaps, they lack confidence. Working as a pair, any given task seems less formidable.

Procedure. A situation is chosen that involves all members of the group. If there is an odd number the tutor should participate. For example:

A sum of £500 has become available. Certain organisations within the community are eligible to benefit. A representative from each of these organisations has been invited to attend a meeting to determine how the money will be distributed. The meeting is chaired by the person who will make the final decision.

Doubling method is explained.

Students pair up.

Each pair chooses their organisation and, to avoid duplication, declares their choice.

One pair is asked to be in the chair.

Time is allowed for preparation.

Interaction begins when preparations have been completed.

Teaching points

It may be necessary for the tutor to give some help to the pair allocated responsibility for chairing the meeting. It is advisable not to cut down on preparation time. To sustain the exercise at a worthwhile level, cases have to be well thought out.

Although, as will have been recognised, Doubling is quite artificial in concept, it provides students with the opportunity to engage in an exercise which can be most enjoyable and at the same time give insight into behaviour at group meetings, case conferences, staff meetings, etc. where people are often seeking to get the best possible deal for themselves or for the persons they represent.

It is a method of working which involves everyone, possibly more actively than if half were engaged in the interaction and the other half observing. Those who are in the silent chair require to listen carefully to all that is being said so that they may offer the necessary support as and when required.

In life quite often the individual person becomes so involved in the presentation of his own argument that he fails to appreciate that it is cutting no ice with the others present. In doubling the *alter ego* is in a position to notice if this is happening and maybe as a consequence comes to a better understanding of the skills required for the effective presentation of an argument or point of view.

In the early stages of training for interviewing or case work, the Doubling technique can be most helpful.

FIRST VARIATION

Select the simulated situation. For example: The school youth worker has been asked by the head teacher to visit the home of a pupil who has been in serious trouble.

Cast one student in the role of parent.

Cast two students in the role of school youth worker. (A1 and A2.)

Interaction begins with A1 playing the role.

As interaction proceeds and if A2 wishes to take over she taps A1 on the shoulder and the change is made.

A1 may resume the role by the same procedure.

Note. The parent should be played by the same person throughout.

SECOND VARIATION

Select the simulated situation. For example: The leader of a voluntary organisation has asked a member of the organisation to see him to discuss some important issue.

Cast one student as the leader and another as the member.

Interaction begins.

Observers follow interaction and if any one observer wishes to take over the role of leader the switch is made.

Note. A switch occurs only if an observer considers that an improvement in performance might be made.

If there is within the group a sense of each person being dependent upon the others for help and encouragement to maximise learning there will be no loss of face and no feelings of being supplanted. On the other hand if the Doubling device is regarded in any competitive way this is completely to misunderstand the intention, and will do more harm than good.

This Section concludes with accounts of how role-play was used with young people to promote social skills.

The tutor in the first account was the leader of a youth club and in the second the persons in charge were post-graduate students. It will be noticed that in the first situation the teaching was implicit, in the second explicit. But in both the tutors started where the young people were.

FIRST SITUATION

The leader of a youth club was concerned to ensure that the young people coming into the club, from a rather depressed area of a large city in England, should find pleasure in the club. At the same time he felt that it was part of his function to help them develop greater composure. He set himself the task of trying to provide opportunity for the members to learn to play a more confident social role. He started talking to members singly and in groups and introducing subjects not normally brought up in their conversations. (None of the members knew that he had embarked on a deliberate programme.) Towards the end of that year he suggested that they have a club dinner. The idea appealed. Staff and members of committee organised the meal and decorated the hall and the tables. It was an attractive setting. The girls arrived dressed up and some of the boys also made an effort to be smarter than usual. The dinner was not a success. As the leader said, 'Some of the girls were too overawed to eat, and the boys lit their fags from the candles on the tables and went to the loo when they felt like it.'

The leader continued with his policy. The last that the present writer heard of this experiment was that a highly successful dinner had taken place. Prominent local citizens had been guests. They were received in an ante-room by the members' committee. Sherry was served. At an appropriate moment guests were invited to take their places for dinner. The menu consisted of five courses with wines. One of the club members acted as chairman and piloted everyone skilfully through the toast list.

Teaching points

With the cooperation of interested persons coming into a club to attend functions or to sit and chat, young people have the opportunity to become more confident in conversation and in relations with older people.

This is, of course, a gradual process and must be undertaken carefully. It would be likely to backfire if members felt that they were 'being got at to behave better'.

Learning to play a more confident social role often happens within the confines of the family but this is not necessarily always so and, as with the leader in the club to which we have been referring, the need can be the responsibility of the youth club.

It is interesting to note that the leader operated in the real-life situation. He went into the world of the young people and while they played their real life role he also was playing his but quite consciously and with specific objectives.

SECOND SITUATION

This is an account of work done by two students operating together in a Scottish List D School for Girls (a school for children who need care and protection). The students were newly qualified primary teachers taking an additional qualification in youth and community work. The students had been introduced to role-play and were interested in the practical application. It was suggested to the students that if they wished to introduce pupils to simulation they should begin where the girls were and respond to any opportunity that arose.

STUDENTS' RECORD OF WORK

On our first visit to the school we joined the girls in the recreation room where one particular group was engrossed in trying to 'call up the spirits' while others were sitting around knitting, reading or chatting. We spent some time in the room with the girls. Eventually we asked for volunteers to make up a group that would work with us, having realised that any commitment by the girls should be voluntary. There were eight volunteers including most of the girls who had been involved in the 'spirits' play. The headmaster had previously placed a room at our disposal. Thither we took the girls. We pushed back the desks and formed a circle with the chairs, hoping to help the girls to appreciate that they were not going to have a classroom lesson. We talked to the girls for a bit about this and that, gradually trying to get the conversation into more serious areas. When we felt it appropriate to do so, i.e. when we thought we might get worthwhile responses, we asked the girls to write down on a piece of paper the question which they would most like to have answered. We suggested that to preserve anonymity names should not be put on question papers. Questions were gathered in, placed in a box, drawn out one at a time and discussed. Here are the questions as written down by the girls.

(1) Why would they not leave me down in England when I run away from home?
(2) Is there really reincarnation?
(3) Why are we only allowed a visitor every month and not every week?
(4) Why am I so daft on boys, or should I say that I pretend I love them? I do like them but not as much as I make out.
(5) How can a tomboy act like a lady when she has acted like a tomboy all her life?
(6) What will they do with me because I am not going back to my mother? I have not to speak to her on leave.
(7) Why do the staff stay on here although they get cheek? Sometimes it is very hard for them.
(8) Why do my Mum and Dad hate me?

The main point of interest for us during this meeting was getting the girls to talk simply and naturally about their likes, dislikes, hopes and fears. By the end we felt that the girls had enjoyed their work and certainly during discussion of the questions most of the girls talked easily and seemed sufficiently secure in our company to make their thoughts known.

We discussed what we would do at the next meeting in the light of the following points we had observed and questions that arose in our minds:

(1) Was the game of calling up the spirits a reaction to boredom signifying the need for excitement?
(2) Were the questions indicative of strongly felt emotions or just what they thought we would expect them to write down?
(3) There was, however, a very strong emotional content within the questions, all of which were written down independently.
(4) In the discussion great importance had been attached to personal appearance.
(5) Most of the discussion time had been spent on question no. 5 (the tomboy one) and on no. 6 (the uncertain future.)

On the basis of these observations we decided to try to use simulation with the group next week. We chose the 'tomboy' question. We considered that some of the other questions might lead to emotional involvement, which could lead to a situation we might be unable to control. We thought also that certain other questions might involve us in a ventilation-of-grievance session about the staff which would be inappropriate.

We further agreed that the simulated situation should be a mannequin parade. In such a game, instruction on behaviour would be given to mannequins, not to the girls as pupils in a school. To the next meeting with the girls we took: (1) Items of costume from the college theatrical wardrobe; (2) street make-up; (3) paper tissues; (4) clothes brush; (5) a selection of records; (6) brush and comb; (7) nail varnish etc; (8) coat hangers; (9) our plan for the game.

Briefing to the girls. 'You are all at a school. It is not your own school but a school for mannequins. All of you have entered the school to train as mannequins and we are your instructors.'

Roles were assumed easily and the situation entered into with keen anticipation. It then followed this pattern.

(1) *Walking and Deportment.* (a) walking round the room; (b) discussion on points to look for e.g. carriage, head held up, shoulders back, length of step etc; (c) practice for improvement.

Voice of one of us (styled Directors) 'Very nice, Jean, Head up, Mary. Good, well done. Now smile—lengthen your step, etc.

(2) *Sitting.* (a) discussion on points to look for, e.g. how to cross legs. Suiting position to garment worn; (b) practice.

Directors offered advice.

(3) *Personal Grooming.* (a) hair, (b) make-up, (c) nails, (d) personal freshness, (e) final touches.

Instruction was given with students grouped round Directors. One of us acted as a model while the other made the various learning points.

(4) *Showing clothes.* (a) discussion, e.g. pleasant manner; (b) hang of garment, use of clothes brush and clothes hanger.

(5) *Choice.* We had placed garments on hangers and these were displayed. The girls made their own choice.

(6) *Preparation for the parade.* The mannequins were asked if they would like to put on a mannequin parade for the remainder of the pupils and staff. They were keen to do so. So one of the students went to the headmaster with a request that the other girls and members of staff be allowed to come and see the parade which would begin in about fifteen minutes. (Previously we had spoken to the headmaster seeking his approval, if the request were to be made.)

While the student was away: records were selected; seating for the audience was arranged; order of appearance of mannequins was determined; mannequins added last minute grooming touches.

The audience assembled. Music played softly in the background.

(7) *The parade.* One of us was in charge of the record player. The other described each outfit as it was displayed by the mannequin. The audience enjoyed the parade so much that the mannequins were asked to do it again. The mannequin parade finished at 10.00 p.m. The girls had worked for just under *three hours*.

We were amazed at the vividness of the girls' imagination. They assumed their roles

7

very quickly and were completely involved in the simulation. Apart from one girl (and even she improved as the work progressed) the response to the first exercise was immediate and from then on the girls moved easily from point to point, often anticipating the next instructional step. They used the available space well, giving the impression of self-confidence. The atmosphere throughout was one of enthusiasm, excitement and anticipation. The outfits were chosen without argument and without disagreement.

We asked ourselves these questions:

(1) Would the behaviour discussed and practised in the mannequin parade have any relevance for the girl who had asked the tomboy question?
(2) Would the work make any lasting impression on the girls?

We discovered on later visits that:

(1) Two of the girls had baths for our visit the week after the parade.
(2) One of the girls who was quite plump went on a diet the day after the parade and lost eight pounds in just over a fortnight.
(3) The girls noticed a difference in the behaviour of the girl who had asked the tomboy question, especially at meal times and when she was sitting watching television.
(5) The girls had loved dressing up.

From that night forward until the end of term, when our visits had to stop, all the girls made a point of saying 'Goodnight' and 'Thank you' to us as we left.

Teaching points

1.   The term role-play was not used and the device was not described.
2.   Students began by encouraging communication.
3.   From the questions discussed by the girls, the students chose to develop one that was safe to handle in that it did not involve pupils in emotional interaction.
4.   The students suggested an exercise which they considered would appeal to the girls because of its novelty and glamorous connotation.
5.   The students did not set out to correct behaviour nor to impose recommended behaviour upon the girls.
6.   Their main concern was to engage pupils in an activity which would be beneficial and above all enjoyable.

Footnote

Tutors with considerable experience of using role-play can become rather conservative in approach but by giving students an opportunity to introduce their own ideas and their own methods of working they can avoid this danger. Many tutors will acknowledge on reflection that students have extended and enhanced their repertoire of ideas for role-play.

Following the theme of extending a repertoire, in Part Three scripted role-play and finally educational games are described.

PART THREE

There are two sections in Part Three. In the first, scripted role-play will be described and its usage considered in relation to social work practice and in the training of committee procedure, while in Section Two educational games provide the area of interest.

PART THREE: SECTION ONE

SCRIPTED ROLE-PLAY

It has already been stated that in a role-play participants interact spontaneously: all the information and exercises given in previous chapters have been based upon that assumption. Role-playing that relies on a script will now be described. In certain circumstances this different way of working may be more useful for the tutor than spontaneous role-play.

In this section
(1) the term Script will be defined; (2) the organisation of scripted role-play will be described; (3) circumstances will be listed in which scripted role-play may be preferable to spontaneous role-play; (4) methods of working will be described; (5) examples will be quoted.

1. DEFINITION. The script is not a dialogue committed to print for memorisation and accurate repetition as in the theatre. It is a pattern of interaction which role-players are asked to follow. For instance:

Mrs Black has been in touch with the Social Work Department. Problem, rent arrears. A social worker made two visits to the Black household but on neither occasion did she meet Mr Black. As the social worker considers it important that she does meet him she has decided to call at the house unexpectedly at a time when she thinks Mr Black will be at home.

Script: Social worker arrives at the house. Mrs Black opens the door, is flustered when she sees who it is. She keeps the social worker talking at the door for some minutes, making excuses for not asking her in. The social worker persists and eventually Mrs Black does allow her to come in. Mr Black is watching television. Mrs Black draws attention to the social worker. He is surprised to see her and resentful—'What are you doing here? No one sent for you.'

The script should continue along these lines with actual dialogue being used only when necessary to ensure that key statements are made. Role-takers need not follow the exact wording: this may be paraphrased so long as the sense of the statements remain. It is not normal for scripts to be in evidence during the actual role-play. The practice of having a 'dry-run' ensures that a script can be followed in an apparently spontaneous manner.

2. ORGANISATION. Scripted role-play follows the same sequence as spontaneous role-play, i.e. briefing; interaction/observation; discussion. During briefing, however, additional work is done. The script is prepared and

written down. Copies are issued to the role-takers, giving them sufficient time to become familiar with the required interaction. It is often helpful for the role-takers to rehearse, helpful because it allows participants to become familiar with the sequence of events that each will be required to follow in the role-play at the training session. This rehearsal is not an opportunity to polish up a performance as would be the case in the theatre. It is, rather, an opportunity to ensure that the interaction goes according to the prepared plan. The terms 'dry-run' or 'dummy-run' are often used to avoid theatrical overtones.

3. USAGE. A tutor may choose to use scripted role-play in preference to spontaneous role-play for one or other of the following reasons:

(1)   to recreate a specific set of circumstances;
(2)   to confine interaction within specific limits;
(3)   to demonstrate particular procedures;
(4)   to give practice in the playing of roles where certain procedures have to be followed;
(5)   to bring to life action that has been set down in a text book.

A script allows a tutor to exercise greater control over the learning environment. Where there are specific lessons to be learned from the past experience of others, or in the playing of a particular role in life, this way of working can be most beneficial.

4. METHODS. Several ways of working are open to the tutor.

First Method. Steps to take:

(1)   Objectives and training points to be made are established.
(2)   Situation brief is prepared. This can be founded on fact or near enough to fact to meet training objectives.
(3)   Script is prepared.
(4)   Copies of situation brief and the script are issued to all members of the training group.
(5)   Time is allowed for absorption of information. This will vary according to circumstances.
(6)   Roles are allocated and role-takers given time for a 'dry-run'. Again this will vary according to the sophistication of the exercise.
(7)   While role-takers are rehearsing, observers are briefed.
(8)   Interaction proceeds along the lines indicated in the script.
(9)   Discussion.

Second Method. Steps to take:

(1)   Situation brief and script are prepared as in first method.
(2)   Roles are allocated.
(3)   Role-takers are given *BOTH* the situation brief and the script.
(4)   Observers are given situation brief *ONLY*.

(5) The role-takers are allowed time for their preparation.
(6) Interaction begins. At any moment in the interaction the tutor arrests action to pose a question to observers, for instance—'What should this role—player say/do now?
(7) Each observer is then required to record his/her own response to that question.
(8) Interaction then continues according to the script.
(9) The tutor may arrest action a second time.
(10) Discussion during which observers' recorded responses are considered in relation to the interaction of the script.

This method is especially useful with those who are in the early stages of learning particular skills. For instance, using the situation above, in the Black household, the tutor might arrest action at the moment when Mr Black has just said, 'What are you doing here? No one sent for you.'

Third Method. Steps to take:

(1) Situation brief is prepared.
(2) Script is prepared to a certain point in the interaction.
(3) Training group is divided into smaller units.
(4) Copy of brief and incomplete script are given to each sub-group.
(5) Sub-groups consider given information and decide how the interaction might develop.
(6) In turn each sub-group plays through the script and on to its own development of it.
(7) Discussion.

Fourth Method. Recorded role-play. Steps to take:

(1) Situation brief and script are prepared.
(2) Roles are allocated.
(3) Role-takers record script on tape.
(4) Recorded role-play is played back in class time.

In the play-back the tutor may either allow the tape to run to its completion before making learning points or arrest the tape at any moment to focus attention on some aspect of interaction.

A pre-recording of a scripted role-play has obvious educational advantages: (a) the tutor knows precisely what is on the tape; (b) the role-play can be repeated as often as desired; (c) the interactants have an opportunity to listen to their own work.

Fifth Method. Same as above but a video tape recording is made, with the added advantage to interactants that they are able to observe themselves in action.

Teaching points

Because a tape is to be used for training purposes the recording of the script must be up to the necessary standard for presentation. This means that in the making there are likely to be several 'takes' before all are satisfied that what is on the tape meets training requirements and is clearly audible.

The script can be as described at the beginning of this section, with only key phrases being written down, or it can be a full script with all the dialogue. Whichever type is used, the illusion of spontaneity should be achieved.

A library of tapes can be built up covering different aspects of social work practice, thus providing tutors with training material as and when required.

5. EXAMPLES. To illustrate the use of scripted role-play, three examples are offered:

    (*a*) an account of how it was used by a team of social workers during a training course for inexperienced trainees;

    (*b*) a script suitable for the teaching of committee procedure;

    (*c*) a full script for recorded role-play.

EXAMPLE A. Teaching team: Five social workers—Allan, Beth, Carolyn, David, Ethel.

Training Group: Inexperienced trainee social workers.

Objective: To highlight some of the problems which the trainee social worker may encounter when interviewing clients in their own homes.

Preparation. The teaching team met and agreed that:

    (1) A known case history would be used with certain particulars altered in the interests of confidentiality.

    (2) Alan would prepare the case history and the situation brief.

    (3) Once these were available, Ethel and David would prepare the script.

    (4) Roles would then be allocated.

    (5) Alan would introduce the training programme.

    (6) Copies of the case history would be issued to trainees at the beginning of the session. They would be given five minutes to read it.

    (7) Alan would then point out features of the situation and answer any questions.

    (8) Alan would explain the educational objectives of the role-play and try to ensure that the trainees were alerted to what they should be looking for.

    (9) Copies of the script would not be given to trainees.

   (10) The teaching team should have a further meeting prior to the training session for a 'dry-run'.

Case history prepared by Alan

The case of Anne Smith.
Name: Anne Smith
Address: 5 Old Flats, Miletown.
Age: Seven Years
School: Miletown Special School
Family: Foster parents—Mr & Mrs Blue and their two children, Jake aged eleven and Meg aged nine.

Problem:　Suitability of Blues as foster parents.

Anne came into the care of the Children's Department at the age of nine months. She had been in a residential children's home until four-and-a-half when fostered with the Blues. At five she attended the local primary school. She was very slow to learn and subsequently was considered to be retarded and showing signs of deprivation. At the age of six Anne was placed in a special school.

The Blues had been considered to be adequate as foster parents.
Material standards were not high but it was felt that their home atmosphere was good and that Anne would get the necessary care and attention. Anne was placed with the Blues. Reports on follow-up visits by Miss Brown, the social worker in charge of the case, stated that the house was not as clean as it might have been. Mrs Blue stated that Anne was settling down well. Miss Brown was doubtful. Prior to the transfer to the special school Miss Brown had called at the house to discuss the move with the Blues who appeared to accept that the move was in Anne's best interests. However, when Mr Blue remarked that he was not happy about anyone going from his house to a 'daft school', Miss Brown doubted whether in fact everything was going as well for Anne as indicated to her. It was difficult for Miss Brown to make an assessment of Anne's position: when she called she had little opportunity to talk to Anne, who in any event found conversation difficult. At this point in the case Miss Brown became ill and a student on placement was asked to take the case over.

Interaction script prepared by Ethel and David

Miss Green arrives. Door is opened by Mrs Blue. Miss Green introduces herself and explains that Miss Brown is ill and that she is taking over the case meantime. Miss Green asks how Anne is. Mrs Blue gives a guarded reply but says, 'I suppose you had better come in.' Mr Blue is reading a paper. Television is on. Anne is not in the room.

MISS GREEN:　Is Anne out?
MRS BLUE:　She is in her room.
　(Silence. Miss Green tries to engage Mr Blue in conversation and gets short answers. Silence, except for the television.)

MISS GREEN: Do you think I might see Anne?
(Mrs Blue goes to the door and calls for Anne. Television is still on. Mr Blue continues to read his paper. Silence.)

Anne comes into the room and Mrs Blue says, 'This is the new social worker'. Miss Green then tries to question Anne about her school, her friends, etc. Anne is not responsive. She gives one-word answers mostly, or replies non-verbally. Mrs Blue interrupts to talk for Anne. Miss Green tries to ignore Mrs Blue's contributions. Anne edges her way back to the door and finally runs out. Mrs Blue makes no attempt to stop her. 'She's like that always with strangers but when we are alone she has plenty to say.'

Miss Green feels there is no point in staying and closes with, 'Well there is not much I can do just now so I'll go. I shall try and come back next week.'

Roles were allocated: Miss Green, Beth; Mrs Blue, Carolyn; Mr Blue, David; Anne, Ethel.

At the training session. Steps that were taken.
(1) Alan explained the purpose of the training session; handed out the case history; answered a few questions; gave some additional information regarding the Blue family, the school and the neighbourhood.
(2) Alan briefed trainees and asked each finally to write down some of the problems that might face Miss Green as a replacement social worker, and then to record observations throughout the role-play.
(3) Alan indicated what role each member of the teaching team would play.

Interaction. The role-play proceeded according to the script.
Discussion. Trainees were given an opportunity to declare points that each had noted. Members of the teaching team made their observations. Important learning points were high-lighted.

Points that were discussed included:
(1) The importance of full preparation prior to the interview.
(2) Problems of distractions, e.g. the television.
(3) Factors that made conversation with Anne difficult.
(4) The feelings of a social worker taking over someone else's case.
(5) The problem of getting at the truth of a situation as it affects a child when adults are concerned to conceal the truth.
(6) The technique of questioning young children.

Follow-up. From an initial scripted role-play issues raised can be examined through spontaneous role-play, for example:
(1) Repeat of the initial role-play with different role-takers.
(2) An interview between Miss Green and Anne.

(3) Interview between head teacher of special school and Miss Green.

(4) Meeting between Miss Green and Miss Brown as Miss Green hands back the case.

It is useful on occasions to take a case history and recreate the interaction that did occur to make specific learning points. Such case histories may come from the experience of the tutor, from members of the group or from textbooks. It can be particularly valuable to take case-histories from textbooks. Used in this manner, role-play becomes an extension to reading.

EXAMPLE B. COMMITTEE PROCEDURE. Organisations establish rules for the conduct of their meetings. Persons attending meetings are required to abide by these Standing Orders. The chairman is given powers to control meetings and to ensure that business is conducted according to procedures laid down in Standing Orders. In addition limits are set upon oral contributions and these are often required to be couched in specific phraseology. Because, therefore, there is procedure to be followed, because there are limits within which committee members may operate and technical terms to be mastered, scripted role-play is a particularly useful device for giving beginners necessary practice.

Scripted role-play should follow the exposition of theory. Role-play should be used to give an opportunity to practise procedures of which participants have some theoretic knowledge.

The degree of formality at committee meetings varies according to the circumstances in which they occur. The script should reflect the degree of formality likely to be encountered at committee meetings which members of the training group may be expected to attend. It is better to err on the side of formality rather than informality.

This example of scripted role-play was used with students who had little or no experience of committee procedure but who, in the future, were likely to attend meetings of some formality.

At previous sessions the following matters had been considered theoretically:

(i) technical terms and phraseology used at meetings.

(ii) procedures for (a) convening a committee meeting; (b) preparation of an agenda; (c) dealing with certain items of business.

The following exercise has been designed to put knowledge to the test.

Sequence of Events

1. Tutor's preparation. In advance of the training session the tutor:
(i) devised (a) notice convening meeting; (b) agenda for meeting; (c) minutes presumed to refer to the previous meeting of the management committee of Oldtown Community Centre.

(ii) prepared role cards. Each card gave role, instructions and script.
(iii) gave to students (*a*) notice; (*b*) agenda; (*c*) minutes; (*d*) own role card.
2. Student preparation. In advance of the training session students: (i) checked up on procedures; (ii) noted given tasks and made any necessary preparation; (iii) chairman and secretary met to consult on agenda.
3. Committee meeting.
4. Evaluation.

Information distributed

A. Notice and Agenda

A meeting of the management committee will be held in the Lesser Hall on Tuesday 14 February at 7.30 p.m. It is hoped you will be able to attend.

E. S. Wright
Secretary

AGENDA

Apologies
Minutes of meeting held on 14 January
Matters arising from Minutes
Easter Expedition
Any other competent business
Date of next meeting.

B. Minutes

A meeting of the Management Committee was held in the Lesser Hall on January 14 at 7.30 p.m.
Present: Mr Adam (*Chairman*), Messrs Blue, Brown, Green and White,
          Mrs Jones, Miss Smith, Mrs Wallace and Miss Wright (*Secretary*).
The Chairman welcomed members to the meeting and expressed pleasure at Mr Green's return after his absence due to illness.
APOLOGIES: Apology was intimated on behalf of Mr Gray.

ACTION

1. Minutes	Minutes of meeting held on December 12 were taken as read. There being no corrections adoption was moved by Mrs Jones and seconded by Mr Blue.

ACTION

2. Matters Arising: It was noted that Miss Smith's
                      visit to the Centre at Newtown
                      took place on 30 November
                      and not as originally planned
                      on 24 November.

3. Reports: Mrs Wallace presented an
                      interim report on the findings
                      of the *ad hoc* committee set up
                      to investigate possibility of
                      starting a Lunch Club for
                      senior citizens.

                      It was decided that more
                      information would be required
                      and Mrs Wallace was asked to   Mrs Wallace
                      pursue the matter further.

4. A.O.C.B.   Mr White asked if helpers
                      would be required again this
                      year for Cancer Research
                      Collection. The Secretary was
                      instructed to enquire.   Miss Wright

There being no further business the meeting closed at 9 o'clock.
Next meeting Tuesday 14 February at 7.30 p.m. in the Lesser Hall.

Role Cards

Three examples are given. These are cards for S1 Chairman, S3 and S5
Committee Members.
In the script action to be taken is in bold type.
              action of others is in brackets.
              verbal comments are between punctuation marks.

Card for S1

Role: Chairman.
Prior to meeting consult with secretary S2 (name of student was given) to
agree details, e.g. name of person who has intimated apology for absence and
whether or not any reason was given.

Script

1.   CALL MEETING TO ORDER AT
                      APPOINTED TIME.

2. Apologies   CALL ON SECRETARY TO INTIMATE
APOLOGY
DEAL WITH ANY QUERY THAT MAY
ARISE.

3. Minutes   'Minutes have been circulated so we will take
these as read.'
'Is this a correct Minute?'
(*A correction will be given.*)
DEAL WITH THIS.
'May I now call for the adoption of the
Minutes correct as amended.'
(*A member moves adoption and another
seconds.*)
ENSURE SECRETARY RECORDS
NAMES.

4. Matters arising   'Are there any matters arising from the
Minutes?'
(*A member will raise a point.*)
DEAL WITH THIS.

5. Easter Expedition   'The next item on the Agenda is the
forthcoming Easter Expedition. I call upon
S4. to present her report.'
(*S4 gives report.*)
THANK HER.
'Are there any questions that members would
like to put to S4?'
DEAL WITH THIS.

6. A.O.C.B.   'We come now to the last item on the Agenda.'
'Is there any other competent business?'
(*A member will speak to some matter and
his/her right to introduce the particular matter
will be queried by another member.*)
DEAL WITH THIS.
(*Another matter will be raised. It will not be
queried.*)

7. Closure   CLOSE MEETING. THANK MEMBERS
FOR ATTENDANCE. INTIMATE DATE,
TIME AND PLACE OF NEXT MEETING.

Notes. Go over procedures for (*a*) checking minutes for accuracy; (*b*) matters arising from previous meeting; (*c*) A.O.C.B.—check definition of Competent Business.

Card for S3

Role: Committee Member.
Take part in meeting as and when you wish but note that (*a*) you amend Minutes, (*b*) move their adoption; (*c*) query first item brought up under A.O.C.B.

Script

1. Minutes	'I have one slight correction it was I who moved the adoption of the minutes and Mrs Jones who seconded.' 'In the minute it is the other way round.' *(Chairman will take appropriate action and then call for adoption.)* 'I beg to move adoption of Minutes.'
2. A.O.C.B.	*(A member will raise a matter.)* YOU QUERY THIS. 'Mr Chairman, I received no notice that this matter would be brought up at this meeting and I consider it is out of order.'

Card for S5

Role. Committee member.
You should take part in the meeting as and when you wish.
Note that you (*a*) raise a point under matters arising and (*b*) bring up a second item of business under A.O.C.B. This is competent business.
You neither move nor second Minutes.

Script

1. Matters arising	'Did the secretary find out if helpers were needed for the Cancer Fund collection and if so, how many? *(Chairman will deal with this query.)*
2. Easter Expedition	YOU MIGHT WISH TO PUT A QUESTION TO S4 AFTER PRESENTATION OF REPORT.
3. A.O.C.B.	*(A member will raise first item and another will consider it to be out of order.)* RAISE SECOND ITEM.

'Mr Chairman, perhaps members would be interested to know

. . . .

COMPLETE THIS AND THEN
CONTINUE.
'. . . If any members wish further information
I'll give it to them at the end of the meeting.'

Teaching points

Scripted role-play is useful in the early stages of training if members are unsure of procedures. A script indicates action and provides words to use. This helps members to become familiar with phraseology that can be very confusing at first.

Words given in the script need not be repeated accurately. Alternative phrasing may be used. For instance, words given to the Chairman were, 'May I now call for the adoption of the Minutes correct as amended?' At the meeting the Chairman may say, 'With that amendment is someone prepared to move adoption of Minutes?'

Having served its purpose, scripted role-play can give way to spontaneous interaction. The sequence then would be: theoretical study, scripted role-play, spontaneous role-play.

As each new aspect of committee procedure is introduced into training, the above sequence would be followed. For instance procedures for moving, amending and adoption of Motions are difficult to master. It is a big step to go from knowledge about procedures to spontaneous role-play and therefore the intermediate stage is to be recommended.

Variation

It may be profitable to brief the chairman to make prescribed deliberate mistakes.

What to do. Prepare papers and cards as outlined. Determine mistakes to be made. For example: failure to adopt minutes, or permitting discussion on an item of business after a decision had been reached on it.

Write mistakes into Chairman's script.

Meet all role-takers.

Issue papers and cards to them.

Indicate mistakes Chairman will make.

Emphasise that Chairman's conduct is *NOT* to be questioned by committee members. Have a dry run to ensure brief is understood.

At the training session explain to observers that procedural mistakes will be made. These should be noted for discussion after interaction.

Teaching points

This variation works particularly well with large groups. The committee meeting becomes a demonstration. Subsequently, in small groups, members can practise recommended procedures.

Instead of a 'live' committee meeting, interaction can be pre-recorded on tape or video and played back as a demonstration.

Although the objective here has not been to teach committee procedure it is hoped that the ideas offered will be helpful for those who will do so.

EXAMPLE C. The following script was prepared and recorded on tape. It was used in the context of training in the conduct of problem-solving interviews.

Roles: senior social worker; young, relatively inexperienced social worker.

Situation: The junior comes to the senior with a problem.

JUNIOR: I'd like to talk to you about my work. I'm feeling very dissatisfied at the moment. So many things seem to have gone wrong.

SENIOR: All right—tell me a bit about it.

J: Well, as you know I was put in charge of the people who come in to do voluntary work. The idea was that they'd take some of the load of routine work off my back. Things like typing letters, filing, answering the telephone, but it hasn't worked out like that.

S: I see. What happens then?

J: It usually ends up with me doing overtime to catch up on office routine work and this means I'm neglecting my proper work. I feel that instead of taking proper time with clients I'm rushing through so that I will have time to do the paper work.

S: Are you saying that the voluntary workers are no help to you?

J: I'm afraid that's the position. There are six of them. They are supposed to work in pairs. I've to keep chasing them up because they won't arrive on time. They really are so unreliable.

S: Have you discussed the matter with them?

J: No, I thought I'd come to you first. I've tried to get them to come on time and have complained when the work has not been done.

S: Are they interested in the work?

J: They say they are but I don't know if they are. You see, they keep on making excuses for being late or for having to leave early. It is a bit of a shambles really.

S: You arrange their rota?

J: Yes, there's a pair for each day and each pair works a three-hour shift, 1.00 to 4.00.

S: Have you thought about changing it and perhaps allowing them to come when they are free rather than at a fixed time each day.

J: I did suggest that we might change to mornings.

S: And what was the reaction?

J: They weren't too keen.

S: It's a problem—isn't it. Tell me, suppose you lost all your helpers, could you manage?

J: No, I couldn't. If I lost this lot I would have to try to get others.

S: So you need help but the work of the present helpers is unsatisfactory. How can you get that across to them?

J: I feel that they should accept more responsibility.

S: Mmmph! In what areas? Office work alone?

J: It was help with office work that was needed.

S: Yes, that was so. However, it might well be that your helpers would now like to be more involved with people who come to the office—at the reception desk for example?

J: But they volunteered for office duties.

A: Is there any one person in the team who appears to be the leader?

J: I don't know because I never see them together.

S: Would it be worth your while trying to arrange a meeting to discuss matters with them?

J: I couldn't do that. I couldn't face them all.

S: What do you suggest then?

J: Would you speak to them?

S: Uhuh. Now tell me, who is responsible for the team?

J: I suppose I am but I just don't like the idea of talking to them. One or two are a lot older than I am. Besides, they might not come.

S: Nevertheless, these six ladies volunteered for the work and are still with you. It is possible that they might welcome a meeting. It needn't be formal. What about it?

J: I haven't much of a choice, have I? I could try, I suppose.

S: Right. When will you be able to see them?

J: Not before next week. I could suggest next Friday—for coffee—and see what happens.

S: That sounds OK. Will you let me know how things go?

J: Yes. I'll come and tell you. And thanks.

Teaching point

Such a script could be used equally well for a video tape recording.

PART THREE: SECTION TWO

GAMING

The aim of this section is to give basic information to people with little or no experience of gaming.

Contents   Definitions; simulation; role-play; gaming.

Differences and similarities between role-play and gaming.

Development of these techniques.

'The War Game'—an example.

Advice on the organisation of a game that has been designed.

Some observations on gaming as a teaching technique.

DEFINITIONS

SIMULATION

One dictionary defines simulation as, 'A working replica or representation of a model, for demonstration or for analysis of a problem'. That definition is acceptable if 'replica' and 'model' refer to mechanical objects of one kind or another but perhaps it is unsatisfactory when applied to inter-personal interaction. A more acceptable definition would then be, 'A representation of a real-life dynamic situation.'

ROLE-PLAY

The acting-out of a simulated situation by participants in assumed roles.

GAMING

A simulation exercise that involves participants in analysis, decision-making and action, sometimes in assumed roles. An element, some would say essential, in Gaming is competition—not to determine a winner as in a sporting contest but to determine the most effective strategists.

Can one have a simulation exercise that is neither role-play nor gaming?

A major accident was staged at the weekend. Army, Police, Fire and Medical personnel were alerted and immediately went into action. The incident over representatives from the Services involved met to analyse action taken and to arrive at conclusions.

Training exercise or simulation?

At 10 a.m. the FIRE BELLS RANG and the school filed out into the playground as per instructions.

Fire practice or simulation exercise?
Labelling is difficult and often misleading. Labels are necessary for descriptive purposes but the practitioner may consider that it is relatively unimportant what a device is called, so long as it works.

DIFFERENCES AND SIMILARITIES

No clear line separates role-play and gaming. Both could be called simulation exercises and indeed often are. However there are certain differences and these are now described, albeit with some reservation.

Fundamentally role-play is concerned to give participants an opportunity to develop an understanding of specific roles and to increase competence in the performance of them. Major emphasis is upon role-pair-role interaction, and therefore upon relationships. Emphasis in gaming lies less with inter-personal relationships and more with man in relation to his environment and societal systems. Gaming seeks to offer participants opportunities to examine the nature of cooperation in any given task and to develop individual capacity to evaluate, organise and take decisions.

Role-play is a development from the free-flowing activity of play. Gaming has its roots in games where activity is confined within prescribed rules and procedures.

Both role-play and gaming are activity based. Participants are required to think and act on their own initiative and in so doing experience the consequences of their actions.

Other important similarities:

Pre-exercise preparation to determine objectives and the nature of exercise, also to assemble necessary information.
The three-tier structure—briefing, interaction, discussion.
Relevant and appropriate briefing.
Reflection on options and strategies
Encouragement of participants to relate knowledge gained through the simulated exercise to real-life situations.

Both techniques demand much from the tutor not only in their organisation but also in their conduct. Simulations give an opportunity for learning but this can be prejudiced if tutors do not remain sensitive to the capabilities and feelings of group members. These matters have already been discussed fully in relation to role-play and they are equally important in gaming.

DEVELOPMENTS

The acting-out of simulated situations is common practice in childhood. Long before the terms role-play or gaming were known, adults used 'suppose that' or 'let's pretend' exercises in their efforts to advance the learning of children for whom they had responsibility. How did such activities become formalised into techniques? Developments came from different directions. Let us look at them in turn. The acting-out of simulated situations for analysis, increased efficiency and for testing in selection procedures, has been a feature of Army training for many years. Initially such exercises were known simply as training exercises and only later as War Games. It is not too fanciful to suggest that a training method found to be exceedingly useful in the Army was copied, adapted and used in other fields and notably in industry and commerce where there was similar concern to train and develop personnel to maximum efficiency. The title War Game gave way to Business Game or Management Game as appropriate, and the activity proceeded under the generic term Gaming.

A second starting-off point is to be found also within the Armed Forces. When the Royal Air Force developed its Link Trainer the aim was to give potential pilots the opportunity to practise in a replica or model of the cockpit of an air-craft. Teaching through a simulator and simulations was taken up by the BBC and developed into sophisticated programmes to explain to lay-persons tech-nological exploits such as rocket launchings and moon landings. It would seem that the Link Trainer and the BBC models and programmes gave impetus to the development of games for use, in particular, in mathematics and the sciences.

In quite a different sphere of endeavour the psychiatrist J. L. Moreno in his work with disturbed patients was also exploring the possibilities of simula-tion. Dr Moreno encouraged his patients to engage in improvised dramas based on their own problems and to this type of activity he gave the name psycho-drama. Where Moreno led others followed. An increasing number of therapists began to use psycho-drama in the treatment of their patients as an alternative to the one-to-one consultation. Through his writing Dr Moreno expounded his theories. The impact of these was considerable, particularly in the United States. Social-psychologists and sociologists, mainly American, recognising the value that the acting-out of problems could have in the training of professional workers other than therapists promoted the method and gave to it a new name—role-play.

The profession that operates in simulated situations as a matter of course is that of the actor. One could call a scripted play a large-scale simulation. Improvisations, that is unscripted playlets—are used extensively in the training of actors and teachers of drama. Pre-Moreno, those who taught drama in school or college involved their students in improvisations as a means of developing acting ability, but also to encourage self confidence in communication in everyday life situations. It was through the writings of Moreno and from the work of Peter Slade in Birmingham and Brian Way in London that a significant number of drama teachers moved further away from improvisations to role-play with its greater emphasis upon relationships.

Possibly educationalists in the United Kingdom have been slower to accept the validity and potential of role-play and gaming as teaching methods than were their counter-parts in the United States. However, the position in Britain today is that these techniques are becoming well known. Workers in different disciplines use simulation to serve their own particular purposes. Thus, for instance, one finds many examples of the effective use of role-play in widely different circumstances. As for gaming, it features in training courses for business executives and management personnel, in classwork at the top end of a primary school and at any stage in secondary, further and higher education. Both devices are proving to be useful in the context of education in its widest sense.

The following is a practical example of gaming:

THE WAR GAME

This is an account of an exercise in world politics designed by the senior history master at Robert Gordon's College, Aberdeen, and undertaken by sixth-form pupils.

The War Game took place over two schooldays. Those days were each divided into two sessions, making four sessions in all. Each session was a War Game day and each day was divided into twentyfour units representing hours. There was a natural break in the middle of each session.

Obviously there had to be enough to talk about in order to sustain the exercise at the level of world politics and throughout the allotted time.

Preparation. Three months before the Game started pupils were allocated roles and much work had to be done in the studying of roles. In addition, students had to have a fair knowledge of international affairs in general, and a detailed knowledge of the internal affairs of their assumed country.

Much thought was given to the mechanics of the game. It was agreed by the master in charge and his colleagues that the game would be held in the school hall which, for the duration, would become, in turn, the cabinet rooms of each power, conference room at U N O and a bird's eye view of the world in action. It was decided, also, to use a tape recorder and overheard projector to feed into the meetings news items and other relevant information.

As the day of the War Game approached the problem of how to start action exercised the minds of the organisers. The possibility that the game would turn out to be an anti-climax or, worse still, a flop was very real and produced anxious moments. It was finally agreed that to avoid such dangers pupils would require to become involved in the reality immediately and that this might be achieved if the first news flash gave word of a human rather than a political story. An appropriate one was devised.

On the appointed day, the boys in their assumed roles assembled in the school hall and took their allotted places, country by country. Suddenly everyone heard an announcement. The game was on. This 'BBC' announcement was followed by an eye-witness account of an attempted escape from East to West Germany. The Heuss family, while trying to escape, were caught in no-man's land. One of the children was gunned down and lay in full view of both sides. Neither side would let the other move. From this introduction and the feelings the incident aroused, the exercise gathered momentum. News items and relevant information from the various trouble spots were fed into conference sessions. Thus when, for example, politicians were discussing the question of the Berlin crisis, news of the bursting of a large dam in Central Russia would be flashed across the screen. In the light of every new piece of information a different aspect of world or national affairs would command attention. At the end of the War Game the point was reached where China and USA were on the brink of war over the question of Formosa.

COMMENTS BY THE MASTER IN CHARGE

History obviously lends itself to this kind of treatment. It is much more satisfying for the older, more able, pupil than the re-enactment of scenes from the past in which the outcome is already known. It provides a first class training ground. It requires considerable research into facts and characters; soaking in of such knowledge; reflection on what has been acquired; and then the exercise of that knowledge in action confined and disciplined by the limitation of character and situation.

The whole exercise as well as being informative, was rewarding, challenging and, above all, enjoyable. It brought the boys to a feeling of reality difficult to achieve in conventional ways; it touched their emotions, sometimes unbearably and it made them realise the truth of the phrase that 'politics is the art of the possible' in a way that would not have been possible by any other study in school.

I would have no hesitation about repeating the experiment. I entered upon it with great trepidation and anxiety but it proved a real highlight for the year particularly coming in the last week of the summer term.

COMMENTS BY PUPILS

Pupil A

From the point of view of the participants, The War Game was an unqualified success as it not only provided an opportunity of experiencing the chaos and complexities of international relations but also proved to be thoroughly enjoyable.

I found myself in the role of Foreign Minister of Red China, and so it was necessary to submerge my own political instincts and to adopt the attitude of a fairly extreme Communist. The value of the exercise was immense in that one grew more and more sympathetic with the character one was playing as one had to deal with the seemingly endless problems which cropped up. Only after participation did I begin to appreciate the immensely difficult tasks with which the world's leaders are continually confronted.

Pupil B

During the game one had the impression of confusion, of how rumours spread like wildfire and how difficult it was to ascertain what was happening. Was this what power politics are really like? We are assured that it is. No wonder the world has to meet so many crises. We were all impressed by the reality of the exercise. People seemed to lose their own individuality and become like the assumed person in word and thought.

When the War Game was over, our first reaction was one of relief and then of annoyance that it was over and we had not done all we had set out to do. We sat down and began to unwind. We had not arrived at any simple solution for the problems of the world but we were far more acutely aware of international relations and of the delicate balance of international peace.

Pupil C was asked questions.

Q   Did pupils find it easy to assume roles allocated to them?

A   Yes, fairly easy, though of course there are a number of qualifications; Firstly, it depended on who the politician was. If he happened to be a forceful character or a well-known figure the task was much easier. It was more difficult when the character was enigmatic or colourless. Secondly, a lot depended on the character of the pupil and his attitude to the exercise. Luckily most people made a serious attempt to study their roles, but in cases where the preparation was not sufficient this proved to be a handicap which no amount of goodwill could surmount.

Q   How did shy boys respond to such an exercise?

A   Thanks to excellent management, there was really no problem here. Shy people were given unspectacular but still important roles. They became personal secretaries and cabinet ministers or the equivalent rather than national leaders. Perhaps, indeed, things would have gone even better if we had all been shy! The atmosphere would certainly have been more diplomatic.

Q   Was the exercise valuable?

A   The exercise was extremely valuable, quite apart from being most enjoyable. Its value could not of course, be assessed in concrete terms except inasmuch as we all learned a lot about world affairs, diplomatic procedures and the conventions and contributions in terms of the general interest and awareness it aroused. I'm sure, for instance, that we all read the papers more closely afterwards. It also provided in a small way an insight into problems facing the countries of the world in their dealings with each other. It was particularly apparent to me that one of the barriers to any kind of treaty was a mutual lack of trust. Surely one of the problems we face today.

OBSERVATIONS ON THE WAR GAME

This was a fairly high-powered game but one within the capabilities of the sixth-form pupils.

The game was an extension of class work.

It was designed by the senior history master who had no previous experience of such work.

The study of roles and background information began three months in advance.

All aspects of preparation for the playing of roles, mechanics of the game and the organisation of it were completed before game action began.

Post-game discussion was an important aspect of the exercise.

General points

A game need not be complex. It is possible to have a much simpler game than The War Game both in design and in conduct.

A decision that a teaching programme should include a game should be made only after certain questions are answered satisfactorily.

Among the most important are:

(1) What gains are to be expected from participation?
(2) Are the available resources sufficient for the undertaking of a game?
(3) Would participation over-tax group members?
(4) Would it be a practical proposition from every standpoint?

Making a start

If a tutor with no experience of gaming decides that her pupils will benefit from taking part in a simple game based on class work, two possibilities are open to her. She may design a game for her own use or acquire one that had been designed.

Design

Potential designers should think of a game as an extension of role-play and devise a series of related exercises that will meet training requirements. Inevitably, in the planning and conduct of such an exercise much will be learned and from these experiences tutors may then go on to explore the complexities of designing.

Example. Suppose that a teacher has been studying local government with a class of pupils. She devises a series of related role-plays to give pupils an opportunity to handle knowledge gained in class. A particular problem raised by a group of citizens—for instance, the damp condition of houses—forms the basis for action. Possible role-plays (a) two or three tenants meet to discuss the problem; (b) meeting between tenants and local government official; (c) public meeting; (d) television interviews.

In the section devoted to youth and community work a method of role-play which was entitled Consequences may serve as a useful guide to the organisation of an extended role-play. If this pattern is adopted the teacher will probably discuss with pupils what steps will be taken after each role-play. The necessary briefing and preparations will then be made before the next interaction begins. Again, if this method is used, although some roles will be allocated at the outset, others will be determined as the need arises.

A teacher, however may consider that for a first attempt at gaming she prefers to use a game that has been designed. So let us take a look at that option.

The other option

Having determined objectives:

(1) Consult a catalogue and from given descriptions choose the game most likely to meet requirements. Catalogue entries include: (i) brief description of game action; (ii) aims; (iii) age range for which game has been designed; (iv) min-max persons required to play the game; (v) min-max time required for playing the game.
Note age range, time and numbers carefully and be sure these match requirements. Avoid games that seem complicated in description. Beginners should go for simplicity.

(2) Order from the given address well in advance of the estimated time you consider necessary for preparation.

(3) Arrival of package. A game comes to purchasers with full instructions and all necessary game materials. The package will include:
(i) A teacher's manual giving, probably, (a) notes on simulation as a technique; (b) objectives of the particular game; (c) rules for the

conduct of the game; (*d*) advice on teacher's preparation; (*e*) advice on different strategies that may be adopted; (*f*) advice on briefing; (*g*) advice on de-briefing; (*h*) suggestions for follow-up work.

(ii) Background information on the game topic, perhaps introduced through a filmstrip and/or tape recording.

(iii) Role cards.

(iv) As necessary, charts, pictures, worksheets, maps etc.

(4) Study material

Although the game has already been designed it will require to be adapted to meet the purchaser's specifications and circumstances. This may involve some alterations in role briefs, and reduction or increase in number of players. Whatever adaptions are necessary, they should be made before players are briefed.

The tutor must be as familiar with the Game and its operation as if it were his/her own design. To purchase is not therefore an easy option, but then anyone looking for a soft option would not choose gaming. It can be a most valuable method of working but undoubtedly it is time-consuming.

(5) When adjustments are completed and the game procedures fully understood, proceed to brief participants. This may include showing a filmstrip, or playing a cassette. Also in the briefing it may be necessary to explain procedures, and give time for assimilation of the given material i.e. the charts, maps, etc.

(6) Allocate roles, give out role cards, and answer any queries.

(7) Give time for study and preparation. This includes the individual study of allocated role, and absorption of information given in the briefing.

(8) Check that participants understand assignments and are ready for action.

(9) Proceed with game action.

(10) Post-game discussion and evaluation.

The following observations are directed particularly towards those who may for the first time be considering gaming as a teaching method.

OBSERVATIONS

Like role-play, the technique of Gaming will appeal to some people but not to others. It is more likely that pupils will find the device congenial than students as the latter may be less willing to commit themselves to the demands of a game.

Certain problems are inherent in the technique.

Time. Undoubtedly the biggest problem centres round time. Games are neither easily nor quickly designed. Even if a game is purchased, a considerable amount of time has to be spent in preparation. Although time is needed for the preparation of any lesson, gaming is exceptionally demanding in this regard.

Commitment. The extent to which individuals invest interest in a game varies. Some participants may coast along, leaving the bulk of the work to others. Again this would be a greater problem with students than with pupils. As one of the pupils said in his comments on The War Game, ' . . . a lot depends on the character of the pupil and his attitude to the exercise. Luckily most people made a serious attempt to study their roles, but, in cases where the preparation was not sufficient, this proved to be a handicap which no amount of goodwill could surmount.'

Gaming is a corporate exercise, so the lack of effort from some not only prejudices learning but can give rise to feelings of extreme annoyance among those who have done some work.

Benefits. In certain circumstances, the number of persons likely to benefit from a game may not be sufficiently great to justify the use of the technique. One thinks especially of a game where there are a few key roles and several minor ones. Those playing the key roles will be involved and possibly extended but for those in the minor roles, with much less opportunity to be involved, the experience will not necessarily be as interesting or beneficial.

The decision to introduce gaming into a particular programme of study should be reached after due consideration of resources and demands.

Positive aspects

Positive and negative features co-exist in every teaching method. Therefore although gaming may be seen as a soft option for some participants it can be a useful means of motivating some pupils/students. This is particularly so if a game is introduced into a programme of learning that has followed a traditional pattern.

There are obvious benefits to be derived from gaming. For instance participation in a game may bring about:

    (i)   improved skills in analysis and decision-making;
   (ii) increased knowledge of the game topic;
  (iii) stimulation of interest in matters about which the game is concerned;
  (iv) improved skills in working with others.

Other benefits may accrue, side effects perhaps, but nevertheless equally important.

(i) The relationship between lecturer and students, or between teacher and pupils, may be enhanced as a consequence of their work together in a game.

(ii) The challenge of a game may call forth qualities from participants that have lain dormant.

(iii) The excitement that a game engenders may give impetus to re-appraisal of self and be the source of greater social confidence.

(iv) Gaming can be a refreshing experience for the tutor.

It is not suggested that gaming can or should replace more traditional methods of teaching. Gaming is more in the nature of special expedition than of every-day walking.

As with other teaching methods, gaming may not produce expected or desired results and rewards. Nevertheless through involvement in the problems of a particular game some insight into the world beyond the immediate learning environment can be gained. That in turn may lead to further knowledge of the human condition.

> . . . we may touch understanding
> As a moth brushes a window with its wing   (C. Fry)

CONCLUSION

What I have tried to do in this book is, first, to describe role-play as clearly as possible and to draw attention to the responsibilities and duties of the tutor; secondly, to offer ideas on how the device may be used in different training circumstances. Finally I have contrasted and compared role-play and gaming and offered advice on the design and organisation of a game to persons with little or no experience of this particular teaching method.

It is not easy to adopt a new way of working, particularly one that calls for a changed relationship between student and lecturer, or between pupil and teacher. To be weighed in the balance and to be found wanting is not a comfortable experience, but it is one with which pupils and students are familiar. Thoughts of possible failure should not deter. Skill in the operation of simulation exercises will develop with experience, but a start has to be made for that process to begin.

Perhaps it would be helpful to bring back into focus the four post-graduate students in conversation with their tutor. In the extract recorded in Part Two, the students were discussing their reactions to their first experience of role-play. In the following excerpt they express their views on role-play as a teaching tool and their position as apprentice tutors.

T   Now that you have had some experience of role-play as role-takers and as tutors, what are your views about the technique?

F   I go back to what I saw with these 15-year-olds I mentioned earlier. A role-play of a Children's Hearing* was set up. One of the workers took the part of the offender and the kids were given the roles of Reporter, Social Worker and Panel Member. All the kids at the Centre had gone through the Hearing procedure so they were well aware of what happened. The worker playing the role of offender sat head-down and didn't answer clearly. During the role-play the girl who was chairman

---

* In Scotland, Children's Hearings rather than courts have responsibility for dealing with children under the age of sixteen who are in trouble and who may need compulsory measures of care and supervision. A Children's Hearing is formed by three members of the general public who have volunteered their service and who have received training in the different duties and responsibilities of Panel Members. Also at the Hearing are: the Reporter, an official, often a lawyer, who has responsibility for determining whether a case should be brought before the Panel; also a social worker, who gives a background report. It is considered important that a child attending a Hearing should be accompanied by both parents or guardians. Their attendance has been made compulsory by law unless special permission has been given to stay away.

of the panel shouted at the offender to get his head up and stop mumbling. Afterwards there was a fantastic discussion about this and the kids got so much out of it.

S   Role-play does give some understanding of other people's positions. In a straight discussion the protagonists are quite convinced of their own position. If you are role-playing you can find out what it is that gives the other side its conviction.

B   I think when you role-play you get rid of any fears you had beforehand and afterwards you feel a bit exhilarated.

S   This brings people closer because they have shared the same sort of anxieties about having to role-play.

T   Are you saying that it has a social value apart from an educational one?

B   Yes, but it has personal value also.

L   It does help confidence.

T   What about yourselves as tutors?

B   I didn't plan my first exercise at all well.

S   But there is some danger in over-planning. It is important that the energy should come from the persons taking the different roles. You are really asking them to act on their own initiative so you shouldn't give out too much information.

T   What's too much?

L   You need to give people enough information for them to believe in the role and to take it on but if you supply too many details a person playing the role might try to reproduce what the tutor had in mind.

F   Briefing should not be restrictive.

T   What appeal has role-play for you as a teaching method?

F   I would eventually want to use role-play but at present I'm not sure how to handle it—particularly in the discussion stage but I do think it could be very, very useful. By the end of the course I hope I'll have things sorted out in my mind.

S   I can imagine when you are used to role-play it could be a great deal of fun—But maybe then it becomes something different?

T   Not really—because you learn from fun and maybe that's a good note to end on.

The students in the above conversation had opportunity to practise the role of tutor in college. With persons already in post, rather than begin with their own pupils or students, they may wish to persuade two or three friends to be their guinea pigs.

I hope that the information contained within this book will lead to a fuller understanding of simulation techniques and will tempt readers to explore possibilities in their own training programmes.